MW00782000

"*Cultural Catholics* is a very readable and engaging look at that half of the U.S. Catholic church on the margins or totally outside of parish life. Maureen Day digs into the subtle issues of cultural Catholics versus active Catholics with a sensitive sociological and pastoral eye. She highlights the critical question of 'who' mediates the Church—be it parishioners, parish staff, deacons, or priests—and how those on the margins experience this mediation. Includes lots of pastoral insight and suggested actions."

—Tom Gaunt, SJ, Executive Director, Center for Applied Research in the Apostolate (CARA), and editor of *Faith and Spiritual Life of Young Adult Catholics in a Rising Hispanic Church*

"For anyone who cares about the Catholic faith surviving, is willing to imagine a new way of defining a 'lived faith,' and is enthused by the idea that there is a new path forward for Catholic identity, this book is for you! This research and its application help all of us in church life to reframe our understanding of the role Catholic identity plays in the lives of so many and encourages us to be innovative in how we respond to the concept of 'cultural Catholicism' as a positive starting point. In this light, all of us can be considered 'cultural Catholics' anew, and I am hopeful for the path forward."

—Nicole M. Perone, National Coordinator, ESTEEM, Chair of the Board of Members, National Institute for Ministry with Young Adults

Cultural Catholics

Who They Are, How to Respond

Maureen K. Day

LITURGICAL PRESS
Collegeville, Minnesota

litpress.org

Cover art courtesy of Getty Images.

© 2024 by Maureen K. Day
Published by Liturgical Press, Collegeville, Minnesota. All rights reserved.
No part of this book may be used or reproduced in any manner whatsoever,
except brief quotations in reviews, without written permission of Litur-
gical Press, Saint John's Abbey, PO Box 7500, Collegeville, MN 56321-7500.
Printed in the United States of America.

1   2   3   4   5   6   7   8   9

Library of Congress Cataloging-in-Publication Data

Names: Day, Maureen K., author.
Title: Cultural Catholics : who they are, how to respond / Maureen K. Day.
Description: Collegeville, Minnesota : Liturgical Press, [2024] | Includes
    bibliographical references and index. | Summary: "Cultural Catholics
    tells the story of those who consider themselves Catholic, but infre-
    quently attend Mass. This book examines cultural Catholics on a range
    of topics and offers ministerial insights for connecting with and accom-
    panying them on their spiritual journeys"— Provided by publisher.
Identifiers: LCCN 2024013866 (print) | LCCN 2024013867 (ebook) | ISBN
    9798400800702 (trade paperback) | ISBN 9798400800719 (epub) |
    ISBN 9780814689615 (pdf)
Subjects: LCSH: Catholics—United States—History—21st century. |
    Christianity and culture—United States—History—21st century. |
    Catholic Church—Customs and practices.
Classification: LCC BX1406.3 .D395 2024 (print) | LCC BX1406.3 (ebook)
    | DDC 282/.73—dc23/eng/20240513
LC record available at https://lccn.loc.gov/2024013866
LC ebook record available at https://lccn.loc.gov/2024013867

To my kids and godkids: Addie, David, Iris, Mariana, Marisela, Micah, Noah, Tammy, Veronica, and Vitale. May you always know that you belong!

Contents

Acknowledgments

I have tremendous gratitude for the many people and organizations who began, maintained, and helped disseminate the findings of this national project. Beginning with the funders, I thank the Louisville Institute, the Anderson Foundation, the National Catholic Reporter Publishing Co., Alfred & Kathleen M. Rotandaro, Kevin J. Healy, and the Kathleen Blank Reither Trust for their generous gifts supporting the administration of the 2017 survey. Thank you so much for recognizing the importance of research on American Catholic laity; I hope you find this deep dive into the data on cultural Catholics to be a worthwhile read with far-reaching implications.

Major thanks go out to editorial director Hans Christoffersen and the responsive team at Liturgical Press. You had interest in this project from the outset and I felt your enthusiasm throughout the writing process. From giving initial feedback to improve my proposed outline to designing an attractive cover to fine copyediting, your professional expertise helped produce an incredibly polished book. Thank you for your attention and guidance with both large-scale suggestions and better comma placement!

I also want to thank my institutions and colleagues. First, I thank my various academic homes: the Franciscan School of Theology, the Center for Religion and Civic Culture at the University of Southern California, and the Institute for Advanced Catholic Studies, also at the University of Southern California. I appreciate the collegiality, conversations about the data and findings, and the many ways my institutions directly and indirectly supported this project in its various phases. I also want to acknowledge my students . . . you are absolutely the reason I got into this gig! And even though I'm on the other side of the desk, you still constantly teach me new things. I hope that you see that your pastoral experiences, concern for those to whom you minister, and professional insights shine through here! A special shout-out to one of my students in particular, Brian Frulla, whose MDiv capstone project on evangelization pointed me toward some additional resources on cultural and former Catholics that helped me in thinking through the data. Also, my thanks to my extra-institutional colleagues, especially those whose research informed this work.

Huge thanks go out to the over 1,500 Catholics who agreed to take part in the national survey and share their responses on a variety of beliefs and practices related to Catholicism. In wave after wave, your experiences as "everyday Catholics" were incredibly informative to a wide audience. And for the first time the whole team gets to thank the interviewees—many of whom were familiar with the previous books in the American Catholic Laity series[1]—who said they looked forward to the ways these interviews might enhance our analysis. Even though the interviews were merely used to enhance, illuminate, or otherwise "chime in" on the data for this book on cultural Catholics, your words still offer much pastoral insight and help bring these findings to life. Thank you so much for being generous with your time and experiences, especially given your busy schedules.

I also want to thank those who were important during the research and writing process. Given the focus of this book, special thanks to friends and colleagues in "Catholic-land": Jerome Baggett, Tricia Bruce, Jeff Burns, Jim Cavendish, Kate DeConinck, Michele Dillon, Thu Do, Stephen Fichter, Tom Gaunt, Mary Gautier, Paddy Gilger, Brett Hoover, Matt Manion, Paul Perl, Tia Pratt, Susan Reynolds, Lucas Sharma, Porsia Tunzi, Jonathon Wiggins, and Richard Wood. Thank you not just for your academic support and collaboration, but simply for being people I look forward to hanging out with!

Lastly, thanks to my family. First, to my departed father, whose high commitment to his faith helped get me into this stuff, and to my mom, whose high commitment to everything continues to inspire me. My sister, my niece, my Fuller family: you bring me rejuvenation whenever we gather. To the Czap/Brooks crew: we took lots of vacations as kids, and I am thrilled that we (our parents included!) are getting back into this! My adult child, Veronica, for eighteen years has shared many adventures with us; my heart and hope go with you as you make your own. My teen, David, continues to love me into being through his sweetness and affection; you are awesome! My husband, Joseph, joyfully surprises me as we try new things together; thanks for loving me and for reminding me who I am. You are all my love and my light and my life.

Introduction

It's a warm spring day and Bridget is pushing her daughter, Erin, in a swing at their neighborhood park. Bridget is thirty-nine years old, friendly and easygoing. Between knock-knock jokes, she checks the time on her cell phone; she doesn't want to be late or too early for Erin's swim class at the city pool. Erin is in her last year of preschool and Bridget thoroughly enjoys spending time with her on the weekdays. On weekends, Erin stays with her father while Bridget works the weekend shift as a nurse at the local hospital. Although they lived together the first two years of Erin's life, Bridget and her co-parent never married and are not currently dating; it just didn't work out.

Erin's current preschool includes a Protestant Christian curriculum. However, Bridget did not choose the school based on its religious values. She was attracted to the school because of the strong STEM program it is known for. She was a bit intimidated by the fact that there was an interview process for acceptance. Bridget was told at the application stage that the school only accepted students who come from Christian homes. The staff members explained that they wanted to make sure that there is congruency between what the children are learning at home and what they are learning at school. They said they would hear more about her faith in the interview process.

Bridget was nervous. Aside from weddings and funerals, she had not been to church in years. The first question they asked Bridget was about her religious affiliation. She responded, "Catholic." But the slight uptick in her voice made her one-word answer seem more like a question than a statement. Erin was accepted and the school expected the family to find a church home. Out of a sense of fidelity to her promise, Bridget took Erin to Mass three times over the course of that first year at the school.

For Bridget, attending Mass was both familiar and unfamiliar. Bridget went to Mass regularly with her family growing up; it was rare for them to miss a Sunday. She had her First Communion, too, but dropped out of confirmation after a few classes because she thought it was boring. She thought she would know the responses in Mass but was surprised when she said, "And also with you" and found the rest of the parish responding, "And with your spirit." Things were similar yet different enough, and she really didn't care enough to investigate. However, despite the infrequency of these Sunday visits, Bridget always left with a positive feeling that she'd attended. And this inspired her to turn one piece of Catholicism over in her mind fairly regularly: getting Erin baptized.

She met a friend at work, Veronica, who was born in Mexico, also identified as Catholic, and was also only loosely practicing. Their daughters were the same age, and so they had regular weekday playdates. Veronica brought up the subject of baptism first, saying that she and her husband wanted to get their daughter baptized soon and that they would like Bridget to be the godmother. Bridget joyfully accepted and reciprocated the invitation. They started thinking about where they would celebrate the baptism and settled on Veronica's church, as she attended a bit more regularly.

Things quickly became complicated. Bridget was told that she could not be the godmother because she had never been confirmed; the lay minister was sensitive in offering her explanation, and Bridget completely understood. But could they proceed with Erin's baptism with Veronica as the godmother? Absolutely. They would just need to see Veronica's sacramental records. Veronica explained that she had all of her sacraments in Mexico, had no record of these, and was actually not too sure about the place and years for these events. The lay minister apologized, but said that she'd need those documents to continue the process. Veronica and Bridget thanked her for her time and left the parish. After a few months, Veronica said she found a parish in Los Angeles that allowed those who had received their sacraments in foreign countries and had no records to simply give their word. Bridget halfheartedly agreed to proceed. She'd lost momentum and Erin would be moving to a public kindergarten, so her enthusiasm had dissipated.

Odds are that if you are holding this book, pieces of Bridget's story ring true in your life or the life of someone you know. Bridget may not have been familiar with the term "cultural Catholic," but likely you have heard of it, which is what prompted you to pick up this book. You may already have a definition of "cultural Catholic" in your mind. Although the various definitions may differ slightly from one another, they hold in common a sense that cultural Catholics are more loosely tethered to Catholicism—perhaps because of a waning belief, practice, or identity—than those who are called Catholic without the "cultural" qualification. Still, there is a reason people identify themselves or others with the phrase "cultural Catholic" rather than "lapsed," "former," "recovering," or other modifiers that indicate that one's Catholicism has no personal hold at all (or, if it has a hold, that this is a negative connotation). Unlike the negativity associated with "lapsed" or similar descriptors, the collective experiences of cultural Catholics are likely quite varied. Cultural Catholics identify as Catholic, and yet *something* about their status warrants a modifier.[1] What is this "something"? This book examines cultural Catholics through a range of topics in order to better understand them as well as to offer ministerial insights for connecting with them.

Before proceeding, it is helpful to know exactly to whom this book is referring when using the term "cultural Catholic." Here, a cultural Catholic is one who identifies as Catholic when asked about their religious affiliation and attends Mass less frequently than once per month.[2] The cultural Catholics in these pages report the frequency of their Mass attendance, aside from weddings and funerals, as being either "a few times a year" or "seldom or never." Mass attendance was chosen as an important distinction not only because it is predictive of other beliefs and practices[3] but also because those who do not go to Mass regularly are not closely connected to a parish, which is an important space for contemporary Catholic formation. All told, more than half (53 percent) of self-identifying Catholics nationally qualify as cultural Catholics by this definition. In terms of numbers, roughly 78 million people identify as Catholic, meaning roughly 41 million people are cultural Catholics in the United States.[4] This is a huge number, and yet parish staff will likely have little contact with these people. When Catholics are not frequently in their parishes, what does their Catholicism look like? This book offers an overview of these cultural Catholics. Not only does it provide helpful statistics in understanding this group, but it also compares them to Catholics who attend Mass monthly or more often. This allows us to see the differences and similarities in how cultural Catholics relate to their faith compared to Catholics in the pews.

Importantly, the term "cultural Catholic" should not be understood as an evaluative judgment on infrequently attending Catholics, as though they are somehow "less Catholic" or less dedicated to Catholicism. It is this author's opinion that frequent Mass attendance is incredibly important in building Catholic relationships and in forming a Catholic way of looking at the world. Mass attendance embeds Catholics in the parish, one of the few explicitly and visibly Catholic institutions in the United States. To not attend Mass means having to create new ways of understanding one's Catholic identity and often having few others with whom to do this in any intentional way. It is also unequivocally clear in Catholic teaching that the Eucharist is the "source and summit of the Christian life."[5] To forgo this, especially regularly, is of great consequence in the eyes of the church. But this does not mean that cultural Catholics have had poor formation or are somehow weak in their faith. As others have pointed out, the faith of some cultural Catholics is very strong and they are finding their own ways to live it out.[6] Some have experienced hurt and are navigating this. Others have simply drifted. Yet every "cultural Catholic" in these pages identifies as Catholic, despite the fact that some may consider them lost or otherwise inferior.

I have also opted to use the phrase "cultural Catholic" rather than "nonpracticing Catholic" because, as you'll see, cultural Catholics practice Catholicism in a variety of ways outside of Mass. Although some may argue for a different label and have good reasons for this, "cultural Catholic" is the one I settled on and simply indicates infrequent Mass attendance. I hope that my readers can suspend any judgment of their faith and consider what they might learn from the findings and analysis that follow.

Methods

The findings in this book come from a larger ongoing study of American Catholic life that began in the 1980s, led by sociologist William V. D'Antonio. The most recent survey team included D'Antonio as well as sociologists Mary L. Gautier and Michele Dillon. This survey of adult U.S. Catholics was conducted in April 2017 using a representative national sample of 1,507 Catholics, including an over-sample of self-identified Hispanic Catholics. Importantly, using this sample year gives us insights into the lives of those who were attending Mass infrequently *before* the COVID-19 pandemic shifted Mass-attendance patterns around the world.

Respondents were eligible for inclusion if they self-identified as Catholic when asked about their religious affiliation. Our sample, therefore, does not include those who were raised Catholic but no longer identify as Catholic. Nor does it include those who do not *religiously* identify as Catholic but nonetheless still consider themselves Catholic in some way. The findings on cultural Catholics are compared to their more frequently Mass-attending counterparts (those who attend monthly or more often) throughout the book whenever the data is available. Differences of 10 percent or more can be considered substantive. When reporting numbers that *should* total 100 percent (e.g., the percentage of cultural Catholics belonging to our eight income brackets), these might not total 100 due to rounding.

The interview team—sociologists James C. Cavendish, Maureen K. Day, and Paul M. Perl—identified leaders of Catholic organizations as well as Catholics who are popular authors or regularly featured in the media. The main analysis here comes from the survey data and not the interviews with these leaders. However, as these quotes enhance our consideration of the data, they are included. The leaders are laypeople, cardinals, men, women, prominent public voices, and behind-the-scenes people of influence, and also come from a range of ages and ethnic backgrounds. Only a handful of our fifty-eight interviewees are included here, with the most relevant insights peppered throughout the book.

A Demographic Snapshot

Before looking at the ways Catholicism shapes cultural Catholics, it is helpful to have a quick snapshot of who they are as far as age, race and ethnicity, and other demographic variables. The percentages of cultural Catholics who belong to each group are provided in the text, with the percentages of more frequently attending Catholics in parentheses immediately following each statistic. In knowing data on both cultural Catholics and more frequent attenders, one will know whether cultural Catholics are similar to or different from those in the pews. Again, differences of 10 percent or more can be considered substantive, with differences a bit less than this considered slight.

Just to make sure all is perfectly clear, I will slowly walk the reader through some statistics on when cultural Catholics became Catholic. The paragraphs that follow this one will move much more quickly as they will not have the italicized commentary explaining the statistics. Like frequent attenders, cultural Catholics are most likely to have joined the church as "infants" (under one year of age), with 77 percent (79%) saying this is how they entered the faith. *This should signal to you not only that 77 percent of cultural Catholics joined the church as infants, but also that this is very similar to more frequently attending Catholics, 79 percent of whom also joined the church as infants.* Defining "child" as those who joined between the ages of one and twelve, 15 percent (9%) joined in this phase of their life. *Again, not only does this show that 15 percent of cultural Catholics joined in childhood, but that this is slightly higher than Catholics who attend Mass monthly or more often.* Identical to frequent attenders, very few cultural Catholics became Catholic as teens at two percent (2%); to clarify, the data defines "teen" as those who are 13 to 17 years old. *Two percent of both frequent attenders and cultural Catholics became Catholic as teens.* Finally, cultural Catholics are slightly less likely to have come to the faith as adults than frequent attenders, with six percent (10%) becoming Catholic after their eighteenth birthday. *Six percent of cultural Catholics became Catholics as adults, whereas 10 percent of frequent attenders came into the faith in this life phase.* Although only 8 percent of the total sample became Catholic as adults, it is striking that cultural Catholics were less likely to have entered through the Rite of Christian Initiation of Adults (RCIA), the formal process that welcomes adult converts into the Catholic Church; only 61 percent (71%) of cultural Catholics entered the church through RCIA. *Sixty-one percent of adult convert cultural Catholics became Catholic through RCIA; this compares to 71 percent of their more frequently attending counterparts.* This difference might point to the spiritual efficacy of the more relational and communal process of transformation that is built into the RCIA process.

In addition to reporting when they became Catholic, respondents also said how much Catholic schooling they received as well as the religious affiliation of their spouse. Although there did not seem to be much of a correlation between who became a regularly attending Catholic or a cultural Catholic based on attending a Catholic elementary or middle school, there is a relationship at the level of high school and college. Thirty-eight percent (40%) of cultural Catholics attended a Catholic elementary, middle, or junior high school. This drops to 17 percent (22%) for those who attended a Catholic high school, and decreases even further to 6 percent (13%) of cultural Catholics attending a Catholic college or university. While the rates of Catholic school attendance likewise drop for frequently attending Catholics, it is not as dramatic of a rate as it is for cultural Catholics. Perhaps there is something to be said for institutional embeddedness, learning and practicing the faith beyond an hour on Sundays, creating relationships with peers and adults who are a part of one's faith community and more. The contrast is most stark when considering the faith of respondents' spouse: 60 percent (86%) of cultural Catholics are married to a Catholic spouse. Given the much higher rate of Catholic spouses among frequent attenders, there is a clear relationship between Mass attendance and having a Catholic spouse.

To be clear, all the relationships between the variables and Mass attendance—those discussed here as well as elsewhere in the book—are just that: relationships. We cannot with any degree of certainty claim that one thing *causes* another. For instance, does more frequent attendance at religious services indicate a higher degree of religiosity, which would make it more important to marry someone who shares that religious commitment? Or does marrying a spouse who happens to be Catholic result in two people who find it "natural" to attend Mass on Sundays? Perhaps attendance even brings them closer together, whereas it amplifies division among those of different faith traditions. But even though we cannot identify with certainty which factor causes the other (and each could reinforce the other), it is fair to say that there is a strong relationship between having a Catholic spouse and Mass attendance when the Catholic spouse gap is so pronounced in comparing cultural Catholics (60%) to frequent attenders (86%).

Education and household income—two variables that are correlated to one another—do not demonstrate a strong influence on being a cultural Catholic. Forty-six percent (47%) of cultural Catholics have a high school diploma or less. Twenty-eight percent (22%) have completed some college, and 26 percent (30%) have their bachelor's degree or higher. Turning to income, 32 percent (37%) of cultural Catholic households earn $49,000 or less, 50 percent (48%) make $50,000 to 149,000, and 18 percent (15%) earn $150,000 or more.

Closing with gender, generation, and ethnicity and race, the anecdote that there are more women in churches rings true in our data, as cultural Catholics are slightly more likely to be men. Fifty-two percent (44%) of cultural Catholics are men, and 49 percent (56%) are women. As the parenthetical data indicate, there is quite a gender gap among Catholics who regularly attend Mass, but this narrows to only a 3-percentage point difference among cultural Catholics. There are five generations of Catholics in the sample. The youngest are iGen—sometimes also called "Gen Z"—and were 18 to 22 at the time of the survey, being born between 1995 and 1999. These iGen comprise 7 percent (5%) of cultural Catholics; the reason that so few of this generation is represented in the sample is because at the time of the survey most iGen were minors and therefore not eligible to participate. Millennials are those born between 1979 and 1994 and represent 30 percent (25%) of cultural Catholics. Respondents born between 1961 and 1978 are labeled post–Vatican II; 33 percent (32%) of cultural Catholics fall into this generation. Vatican II are those born between 1941 and 1960 and comprise 26 percent (29%) of cultural Catholics. Finally, the oldest generation are called pre–Vatican II, and these respondents are born in 1940 or before. This generation is shrinking as they pass away and account for 4 percent (9%) of cultural Catholics.

Although these generations are fairly balanced, the two oldest generations lean more toward frequent Mass attendance (despite aging and declining health that would warrant less frequent attendance), and the three youngest have cultural Catholic majorities. Some racial groups show an association with being a cultural Catholic. Sixty-two percent (50%) of cultural Catholics are white, 31 percent (40%) are Hispanic, 3 percent (2%) are Black, 3 percent (8%) identified as "other,"[7] and 1 percent (1%) are two or more races. Cultural Catholicism is more common among white Catholics and less common among Hispanic and "other" Catholics. As the data demonstrate, cultural Catholics share some demographic markers in common with more frequent Mass attenders, and they are also marked by some distinctions.

Order of the Book

This book will explore the beliefs, practices, and attitudes of cultural Catholics in several areas. Each chapter will begin with a composite vignette (or two) like the one of Bridget that opened this book. These are in the strictest terms fictional, but are true in the sense that they are each inspired by one or more people I have talked to personally or have heard ministers or other Catholics discuss from their own lives. Any identifying features have been changed (and so any resemblance to real people is coincidental). The chapters then present the findings from the survey, comparing cultural Catholics to their more frequently attending counterparts. These findings are put into conversation with other studies or theological insights as appropriate. Finally, every chapter closes with questions to help readers think through what they have just read and how they might apply it to their context, whatever that might be.

Each chapter has its own specific focus. Chapter 1 will examine the religious beliefs, sense of Catholic identity, and spiritual practices of cultural Catholics. The sorts of questions covered here include how essential devotion to Mary, care for the poor, and a celibate clergy are to their faith; the extent to which it is important that their future generations remain Catholic; whether they think engaging in certain behaviors, like same-sex relationships, precludes one from being a "good Catholic"; what sources they turn to for moral guidance; the personal importance of their Catholic faith; how often they pray; and their likelihood of leaving the church.

Chapter 2 will outline the political attitudes and behaviors of cultural Catholics. Some of the areas this chapter includes are the extent to which cultural Catholics agree with the bishops' position on the death penalty, their perception of how religion influences public life, how often they volunteer in their community, which political party they identify with, and the role of religion in deciding for whom they should vote.

Even though I am defining "cultural Catholics" as those who do not attend Mass frequently, they still offered their experiences of parish life and opinions of church leadership. Chapter 3 explores their thoughts on whether individuals, church leaders, or both should have the final say on personal issues, like the use of birth control; how connected priests are to their parishioners; satisfaction with Pope Francis, the United States Conference of Catholic Bishops (USCCB), their local bishop, and parish leaders; their thoughts on expanding the priesthood (e.g., to married men); whether the laity should have a say on how parish income should be spent; and their reasons for not attending Mass more often.

Chapter 4 will go over the whole of the data to disaggregate cultural Catholics into two groups: those who attend Mass "a few times a year" and those who attend "seldom or never"; cultural Catholics divide roughly evenly into these two groups. Although neither of these frequencies of Mass attendance is especially often, the data shows that in several areas the first group—who might attend Ash Wednesday, Easter, and Christmas—have a different way of approaching their Catholicism than those who attend even more rarely. Rather than reviewing every question again, this chapter will report only on the differences found between these groups, especially as they reveal distinct pastoral strategies in reaching each.

Finally, chapter 5 will put the whole of the data in conversation with other pastoral and sociological resources, suggesting largely applicable considerations and practices for beginning pastoral outreach to cultural Catholics. This chapter will be especially relevant to Catholic high school and university leaders and parish and diocesan ministers, as well as readers who have friends or family who are not engaged in parishes and want to extend an invitation to become involved.

This brings us to one final thought for reflection before turning to the data. You, reader, were drawn to this book for a reason; you will engage with it more effectively if you are aware of why you are reading it. Maybe you know a fair number of folks you would identify as "cultural Catholics"? They might be close friends and family. But what is the motive to purchase, sit down, and read this book? From my perspective, three potential motivations rise to the top.

First, you want to know more about the cultural Catholics in your life and the ways they engage their faith. This book will satisfy your motivation, but I'd push you to go beyond pure understanding and actually approach the cultural Catholics in your life with the questions that internally surface as you read. Write your thoughts in the margins! A second motivation is that you want to better reach out to cultural Catholics in the hopes of helping them to more deeply encounter God, participate more frequently in the sacramental life of the church, or similar. This book can begin a journey with a cultural Catholic, but remember that your role is to accompany your fellow Catholics, not to assume you have all the answers. As will be discussed in the final chapter, sometimes it is a lack of humility among Catholics or a sense of being judged that distances someone from church life. I hope that this book will give you a fair number of questions for the cultural Catholics in your life and an open heart to hear their experiences. A final motivation might be that you are a cultural Catholic yourself, and you want to better understand how you align with or depart from other cultural Catholics. This book will address this curiosity, as well as give you a starting point for understanding Catholics who are more active in their parishes. This book can engage with all three of these motivations, assuming that readers apply their learning with open minds and hearts. With such a disposition, the fruits of careful reading will be rich dialogue and deep encounter. With this, we turn to the first chapter, exploring cultural Catholics' religious beliefs, identity, and practices.

Concluding Questions:

• Who are the cultural Catholics in your life? Do you know why their relationship to parish life is more loosely tethered than your own?

- What are your motivations for reading this book? What are some reminders you'll want to repeat to help keep your mind and heart open so that you can apply the knowledge you'll gain from this book in a fruitful way? Are there any obstacles you should be mindful of that would hinder your openness or make you defensive?

CHAPTER ONE

Catholic Beliefs, Identity, and Practices

Joseph is forty-two years old and was raised Catholic, and quite strongly so according to most standards. He attended an all-boys Catholic elementary school and high school and happily served as an altar boy throughout those years. In fact, at the end of high school he contemplated being a priest, but when he began his undergrad at a public co-ed college and dated his first girlfriend, he decided marriage felt like a more natural vocation for him. Still, his realization that he was not meant to be a priest did not shake his faith, and he continued to attend Mass regularly.

After college, Joseph landed a job as an engineer. He relocated within his home state and attended a few parishes before finding a church that offered a liturgy that he found personally inspiring. The church did not have a young-adult group, so his engagement with the parish was generally limited to Mass and other liturgical events. In his late twenties, Joseph met Heidi at a friend's wedding. They hit it off right away. Although they lived a ninety-minute drive from one another, they thought that trying this relationship for at least a bit would be worth the commute, given their quick compatibility. Once he started dating Heidi, though, it became harder for him to attend Mass regularly.

Heidi was a devoted Lutheran. She went to services at her church each Sunday, and weekends were their only time to see each other. They started by trying to alternate Sundays at one another's church, but it didn't take long for them to realize that Joseph was invited to participate in Communion at her church, but she could not receive the Eucharist at his. After a few weeks of discussion, Joseph said he would attend service at her church each week. He would occasionally attend the vigil at his parish in addition to attending Lutheran services the next morning, but this practice did not last for more than a few months. Given that his weekend was also filled with chores and connecting with his family and other friends, it just wasn't sustainable. Even though he knew the differences in these denominations' sacramental traditions, his weekend was too full, and the Catholic Mass and the Lutheran service just seemed too similar to warrant attending both.

Heidi and Joseph eventually got engaged, and within a few days they realized they would need to decide which denomination would host their ceremony. Given the Communion consideration, and that all her family would likewise be excluded from Communion, as a gesture of appreciation for the sacrifice Joseph had made to attend her church each Sunday, Heidi suggested they opt for his church and have a Catholic ceremony without the Eucharist (Joseph had seen this several times when he was an altar server). Compromising on their faith traditions was the same sort of conversation over and over, simply centered on a different iteration of the same question: How do we navigate Communion? When they were discussing the religious tradition in which they would raise their children, the Lutheran tradition made sense; after all, by this point, they had established themselves as a solid presence in the congregation, and this way everyone could participate in Communion. Aspects of the faith tradition that did not involve Communion, like naming their children after Catholic saints, were nearly always decided in a way that honored Joseph's Catholicism.

Despite the challenges, Joseph never stopped identifying as Catholic. He still feels like Catholicism is "his" home, no matter where he spends his Sundays. He never fails to miss Mass on any Ash Wednesday (with Heidi at his side) or Christmas Eve when it is a year they are celebrating with his side of the family. Joseph also pops in for Mass on holy days on his weekday lunch hour (but sometimes he forgets these, not having the pre–holy day reminder at Sunday Mass). Heidi encourages him to continue to embrace his faith whenever he can. It was never her intention to pull him away from Catholicism; she simply wanted a place of worship where they could both fully participate. Joseph initially felt a lot of disappointment that they were not able to find a home in the Catholic faith, but gradually, over the years, that disappointment faded. Despite infrequent Mass attendance and frequent service attendance, he still deeply identifies as Catholic.

Again, cultural Catholics religiously identify as Catholic. But many wonder, with their loose connection to parish life, what continues to sustain this Catholic identity. This chapter will explore the religious beliefs, sense of Catholic identity, and the spiritual practices of cultural Catholics.

Catholic Beliefs

Beginning with what cultural Catholics consider to be "essential" to their faith, many items on our survey are important to them.[1] Still, their responses in some areas are much lower than their frequently attending counterparts. There are several questions in which the frequently attending Catholics approach the 100 percent maximum level mark, and in some of these the cultural Catholics are quite high as well. Three-fourths or more cultural Catholics say that "belief in Jesus's resurrection from the dead," "charitable efforts toward helping the poor," "devotion to Mary, the Mother of God," and "the necessity of having a Pope" are "essential" or "somewhat essential" to their "vision of what it means to be Catholic."

Essential Elements of Catholicism. "As a Catholic, how essential is each of these to your vision of what it means to be

Catholic? Would you say the following is or are essential to the faith, somewhat essential, or not essential at all?" ("Somewhat essential" and "Essential" combined):

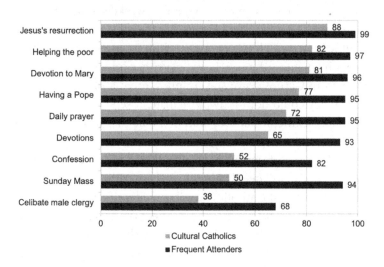

Jesus's resurrection — 88, 99
Helping the poor — 82, 97
Devotion to Mary — 81, 96
Having a Pope — 77, 95
Daily prayer — 72, 95
Devotions — 65, 93
Confession — 52, 82
Sunday Mass — 50, 94
Celibate male clergy — 38, 68

■ Cultural Catholics
■ Frequent Attenders

Smaller majorities—ranging from 50 to 72 percent—say "engaging in daily prayer," "participating in devotions such as Eucharistic Adoration or praying the rosary," "private confession to a priest," and "the obligation to attend Mass once a week" are important to their vision of what it means to be Catholic. The large gap between cultural Catholics and frequent attenders on this Mass attendance item should not surprise us, as Mass attendance is the variable we are using to distinguish cultural Catholics from the comparison group. Still, that half of Catholics who attend a few times per year or less frequently still consider weekly attendance to be an important aspect of Catholicism is striking! The final item, "a celibate male clergy," is considered unimportant by a large majority of the respondents and likewise finds weaker support even among frequent attenders. These findings reveal the elements of Catholicism that are most central to cultural Catholics, many of which do not require frequent Mass attendance to incorporate into or assent to in one's faith life.

"And this beautiful story came out [from someone I was speaking to]. He said the woman told their mentor couple during their marriage preparation, 'I don't attend Mass regularly.' And they said, 'Well, why is that?' And they had established a relationship of trust through previous meals together in conversations, talking about money, talking about life goals. And the woman said, 'Well, I think it's because my mother was overbearing. I just have this side of me, that's just rebelling against her and I just don't want to do it.' The mentor couple then said, 'Would you like us to pray for you in that? That must be very difficult to have those kind of wounds from your mother.' And she said, 'Yes.' And then, just right there, they laid hands on her and prayed this beautiful prayer and tears are streaming down this young woman's cheeks. And I don't know whether there's a happy ending. I don't know whether this woman now goes to Mass every week and now she's a mentor couple. But that woman was evangelized. She experienced the good news of Jesus. She experienced the care of the church in a different way. She's much more likely to come back to Mass and as they have kids and as their kids are growing . . . It's these encounters with more intentional preparation for these significant events, I think, and follow up. We have this window of grace in baptism, marriage, confirmation, RCIA, we have these windows of grace when we're going to encounter people who are not attending Mass or are attending infrequently."

—Jason Simon, President, The Evangelical Catholic

In comparing cultural Catholics with more frequently attending Catholics, there are large gaps as well as amazing consistency in some of the responses, some of which dismantle some "commonsense" understandings about who cultural Catholics are. First, there is a very close alignment with the item that the most cultural Catholics agreed with; regardless of frequency of Mass attendance, both groups of Catholics believed that people "can disagree with aspects of church teaching and still remain loyal to the church." For cultural Catholics, they are likely to see this in themselves; while they do not, for example, follow the church's expectation of Sunday attendance, they may nonetheless consider themselves and others like them to be loyal to the church. For those who attend more often, they may know that faithful dissent is possible within church teaching through preaching or other formation programs at their parish, or, like the cultural Catholics, it could also be known through experience. It should be stated that it is not just total agreement that is similar here; the comparisons across strongly and somewhat agree as well as strongly and somewhat disagree never reveal more than a 3 percent variation between groups.

Agreement with Catholic Beliefs and Practices. "Please indicate whether you strongly agree, somewhat agree, somewhat disagree, or strongly disagree with each of the following statements" ("Strongly" and "Somewhat agree" combined):

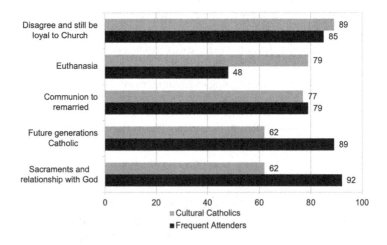

There is a large gap between these groups of Catholics when it comes to their agreement with whether "individuals who are terminally ill and in great pain should have a legal right to doctor-assisted suicide," with 79 percent of cultural Catholics agreeing and only 48 percent of their counterparts saying the same. This is a clear departure with church teaching for cultural Catholics. Looking at Communion for the divorced and remarried, with the publication of Pope Francis's *Amoris Laetitia* (The Joy of Love)—an apostolic exhortation on pastoral care relating to marriage and family life—and the follow-up of the bishops of Argentina, Catholicism made it clear that this was possible. Regularly attending Catholics are more likely to have heard of this pastoral guidance than cultural Catholics. But whether they are guided by church teaching or their own moral sensibilities, nearly equal percentages of cultural Catholics and their counterparts agree that "divorced Catholics who remarry without an annulment should, in consultation with a priest about their situation, be able to receive Holy Communion" at 77 and 79 percent, respectively. As discussed above regarding the first item—remaining loyal to the church while disagreeing with teaching—there was much proportional similarity between these groups when disaggregating the strongly and somewhat agree groups as well as the strongly and somewhat disagree groups.

Although just under two-thirds of cultural Catholics agree "it is important to me that younger generations of my family grow up as Catholics" and "the sacraments of the church are essential to my relationship with God," this is much lower than their counterparts. These both have ramifications for Catholicism. First, with this relatively high indifference to pass on the faith for one in three cultural Catholics, it could mean that for every third cultural Catholic, the faith likely ends with this person. In contrast, with frequently attending Catholics' much higher desire for this, only one-tenth of frequent attenders are nonchalant about passing the faith to their children. Having such a large percentage of cultural Catholics in the United States does not bode well for the intergenerational transmission of Catholicism.[2]

Turning to the sacraments question, a common observation among pastoral ministers is that cultural Catholics are not frequent attenders, but the non-repeatable sacraments of baptism and confirmation, the "rite of passage" of First Communion, and the infrequent sacrament of holy matrimony are moments when these Catholics do approach the church, and sometimes fervently so. However, only 62 percent of cultural Catholics said the sacraments were essential to their relationship with God, and most of these only somewhat agreed with this (20% strongly agreed and 42% somewhat agreed). The wording of the question is also something worth considering: it asks respondents whether the sacraments of the church are essential to their relationship with God; it does not ask simply whether the sacraments are important to them more broadly. It could be that the sacraments are important to many more cultural Catholics than captured here, but their importance lies more in their significance as a Catholic identity marker than as a rite that connects them to God. These people might disagree with the question based on the way it is worded, even though they find the sacraments personally meaningful in other ways. If, as ministers claim, cultural Catholics do indeed approach parishes for sacraments, there are at least two interpretations of this experience. First, sacraments are important to cultural Catholics not as encounters with God, but perhaps as symbols of Catholic identity or as necessary steps toward salvation. So they will, in fact, approach parishes for sacraments even if they chose "disagree" for this survey question as it was posed. Alternatively, it is simply the case that one-third of cultural Catholics do not find meaning in the sacraments. In this scenario, it may also be true that, yes, there are a large number of nonattending Catholics who approach parishes for sacraments, but there are also one-third who simply do not.

"I still think even with people that identify as culturally Catholic, that kind of sacramental imagination that comes forth from the Catholic life and it's hard to shake. Now, it would be interesting to look at the next generation or two generations from now, to see whether that cultural Catholicism holds, to see if people continue to identify as Catholic. I think that's going to weaken going forward. But so these culturally Catholic people presently still have that sense of being Catholic. I've heard people say, 'I'm spiritual, I grew up Catholic, I still identify as Catholic. I really can't go to another religion. I've tried to go to another Protestant or evangelical church, but it's really hard for me because I'm still Catholic.' "

—Sr. Theresa Rickard, OP, DMin, President,
RENEW International

Catholic Identity

A set of questions that more directly taps into Catholic identity are those regarding the beliefs one must hold or the behaviors one must practice in order to be considered a "good Catholic." Here we can see where Catholics draw boundaries as to who does and does not qualify as a "good Catholic." Before going into each item, an overall trend is that cultural Catholics are more inclusive in their boundaries as to the beliefs and practices required to be a good Catholic. But we should also note that even highly active Catholics understand themselves as "good people," a piece of their identity that they readily grant to those outside the tradition.[3] Another important thing to keep in mind is that these responses indicate boundary drawing of the beliefs and practices that place a person within or beyond the pale of being a good Catholic, not what they personally believe or practice themselves. For example, 87 percent of cultural Catholics believe that someone can be a good Catholic without having their marriage approved by the church; this does not (necessarily) mean that these respondents' marriages are not approved by the church.

Two items stand out as being quite important to cultural Catholics: a higher percentage believe a person cannot be a good Catholic "without believing that Jesus physically rose from the dead" and "without believing that in the Mass, the bread and wine really become the body and blood of Jesus." Roughly half of cultural Catholics expect good Catholics to assent to these beliefs. Recognizing that these are central dogmas of Catholicism demonstrates that cultural Catholics have strong commitments to core pieces of their faith. This elevation of dogmas or central doctrines of the faith have been found elsewhere to even unite very liberal and conservative Catholics.[4] It is striking to see, also, cultural Catholics elevate these. Clearly these findings point to the "core" elements of Catholicism that are more likely to be shared by the faithful.

Beliefs and Practices Needed to Be a "Good Catholic." "The following statements deal with what you think it takes to be a good Catholic. Please indicate if you think a person can be a good Catholic without performing these actions or affirming these beliefs. Can a person be a good Catholic" (percent responding "No, cannot be a good Catholic"):

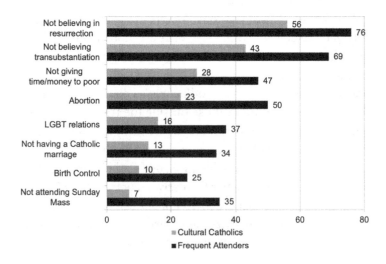

Then there is a substantial leap to the next item, with the subsequent items gradually being seen as less central to a good Catholic's identity. Only 28 percent believe a person cannot be a good Catholic "without donating time or money to help the poor." A mere 23 percent contend that "without obeying the church hierarchy's opposition to abortion" one cannot be a good Catholic. Decreasing still further, 16 percent believe that one cannot be a good Catholic "without obeying the church hierarchy's opposition to gay/lesbian sexual relationships." Thirteen percent say a person cannot be a good Catholic "without their marriage being approved by the Catholic Church." Ten percent (this item is the lowest percentage among regularly attending Catholics, demonstrating its peripheral role in the faith for most Catholics) claim a Catholic cannot still be considered good "without obeying the church hierarchy's opposition to artificial contraception." Nowhere is the respondents' personal beliefs and practices more connected to an item than in the question cultural Catholics find least relevant to being a good Catholic, that is, "without going to Mass every Sunday." As none of these cultural Catholics regularly attend Sunday Mass and, assumedly, many consider themselves good Catholics, it is not entirely surprising that this item should come in as least necessary for being a good Catholic for cultural Catholics.

Cultural Catholics reported the personal importance of the Catholic Church in their lives as well as their likelihood of leaving Catholicism. The Catholic Church is not core to many cultural Catholics, with 2 percent saying Catholicism is "the most important part of my life," 10 percent choosing "among the most important parts of my life," 42 percent responding "quite important to me, but so are many other areas of my life," 35 percent saying "not terribly important to me," and 11 percent reporting "not very important to me at all." The corresponding percentages from frequent attenders were 18 percent, 43 percent, 35 percent, 5 percent, and less than 1 percent, respectively.

Perhaps surprising given the relative lack of personal importance of their faith, cultural Catholics do not report a high likelihood of disaffiliation. When presented with a 1-to-7 scale—with

"1" signaling "I would never leave the Catholic Church" and "7" meaning "Yes, I might leave the Catholic Church," the responses trend toward the lower end of the scale. This is especially impressive given the relative modesty of the "7"; a response of "7" means that someone "might leave," not "Yes, I will be leaving the Catholic Church." For cultural Catholics who even rarely consider disaffiliating, they could easily select the final response as it is written. Instead, 27 percent selected "1," 18 percent chose "2," 10 percent responded with a "3," 19 percent said "4," 12 percent said "5," 7 percent chose "6," and another 7 percent selected "7." The respective figures for frequently attending Catholics, unsurprisingly, skew even further to the lower numbers at 63 percent, 16 percent, 7 percent, 6 percent, 5 percent, 2 percent, and 1 percent. Although the cultural-Catholic likelihood of disaffiliation appears low, being Catholic is also a relatively small commitment on their part. One interpretation of this data is that it is trivial to bother to consider leaving something that is such a small demand of their time and other resources. So although their likelihood of leaving is low, this could be because staying is an easy default given that the cost is not especially significant. This is, admittedly, a glass half-empty interpretation. A more half-full explanation would argue that cultural Catholics are so invested in Catholicism, or that their faith is so steeped into their identity, that they could never consider leaving. Either of these interpretations are plausible. The more half-full explanation probably applies to some cultural Catholics and the half-empty interpretation aptly describes others.

Catholic Practices

To determine the sorts of moral resources cultural Catholics draw upon for discernment, the survey asked which Catholic and secular resources they turned to when faced with an important decision. The first two items are relational—"I talk to a close family member" (81%) and "I talk to trusted friends" (74%)—and percentage-wise are very similar to their regularly attending counterparts. Although the gap between cultural (64%) and frequently attending (90%) Catholics grows when asked whether they "pray or meditate about it," this reveals that a substantial majority of cultural Catholics utilize this faith-based practice when discerning important decisions.

Sources Used in Moral Discernment. "When you have an important moral decision to make, which, if any, of the following activities or sources do you usually look to for guidance?" ("Always" and "Sometimes" combined):

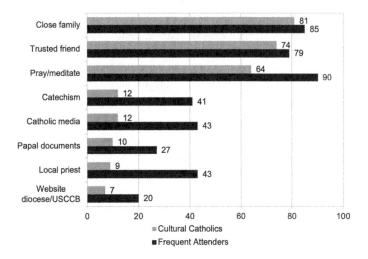

However, ministers who are heartened by the large percentage of cultural Catholics who pray when they have to make an important decision may become discouraged by the other findings. There is a steep drop in the utilization of spiritual resources aside from prayer and meditation. Further, cultural Catholics employ spiritual resources at about one-third the frequency that their counterparts do. No more than 12 percent of cultural Catholics "read the *Catechism of the Catholic Church*," "look at/read Catholic media," "read papal statements or encyclicals," "talk to [their] local priest," or "visit the website of [their] diocese or of the U.S. Catholic bishops" when faced with an important decision. This is not to say that these areas are a waste of resources; in fact, these findings show that some cultural Catholics use these and many regularly attending Catholics avidly use these. However, they cannot be the exclusive or even the primary way to reach cultural Catholics. Although ministers may be somewhat consoled that at least a sizable majority of these cultural Catholics pray, it is fair to wonder how deep, rich, or fruitful their prayer life is without the regular engagement of more developed spiritual resources.

"Our mission statement says that we work to strengthen the faith of practicing Catholics, bring former Catholics back to the faith, and to bring non-Catholics into the church. So, actually that's everybody. That middle group of fallen away Catholics is an interest to us. And the way that we chiefly reach them is through Catholic.com, which is our url. It's amazing, and I'll be happy to tell you a story. But because a lot of people find it, I think that the hierarchy—the bishops and the presbyterate—should look hard at media to reach the lapsed."

—Christopher Check, President, Catholic Answers

The final pieces of Catholic practices this chapter will explore are cultural Catholics' frequency of prayer and confession (neither of these have accompanying figures). Beginning with the frequency of prayer outside of Mass, 7 percent of cultural Catholics pray more than once per day, 25 percent pray daily, 44 percent pray "occasionally or sometimes," and 24 percent pray "seldom or never"; the corresponding figures for frequently attending Catholics are 23 percent, 49 percent, 26 percent, and 2 percent, respectively. Confession is not common among cultural Catholics, with 1 percent confessing once a month or more, 3 percent confessing several times per year, 4 percent confessing annually, 13 percent confessing "less than once per year," and 79 percent confessing "seldom or never"; the corresponding percentages for their more frequently attending counterparts are 8 percent, 22 percent, 20 percent, 20 percent, and 30 percent, respectively.

Concluding Questions:

- Which of the findings do you find hopeful given your ministerial context? Which are discouraging or pose a challenge? Whether hopes or challenges, what might be the opportunities these data point toward?

- What is your own (or your organization's) notion of Catholic identity or what makes for a "good Catholic?" How does this shape the ways you reach out to cultural Catholics? Again, considering your own (or your organization's) notion of Catholic identity, what might be this notion's blind spots that limit or obscure other possibilities for outreach?

CHAPTER TWO

Political and Civic
Attitudes and Practices

It's the day after Thanksgiving and both immediate and extended family members are milling about the house with a jovial attitude and a mild food coma from the previous day's festivities. Some have gone out to do some Black Friday shopping, but most stayed home and to watch football games and classic movies. Leftovers are all that's on the menu and nobody is complaining. The Alvarez family has always been very close and holidays are a special time to gather, whether someone lives across town or is in college across the state. It's a windy day and the final remnant of the fall foliage still clings to the trees. As Cynthia washes dishes, she looks out the window and sees these leaves' desperate act of futility; she can't help but relate this to her faith journey.

Cynthia was brought up in a deeply devout, Mexican American Catholic family and context. She and her two sisters all attended Our Lady of Grace, the Catholic K–8 school down the street. She, the oldest, would walk with her sisters down the street in their blue plaid uniforms and smile as her teachers and friends greeted her upon arrival. She remembers how everyone knew each other, would go to Mass together, would chase each other at parish festivals . . . it was a fun and easy time. The closest Catholic high school was a twenty-minute drive—thirty minutes in traffic—and that was just too far for the family. So she went to the public high school, getting confirmed at her parish in the tenth grade. That was also a positive experience. She got to reunite with some of her elementary school friends for this, and there was a familiarity in praying together. They laughed that they even missed the blue plaid uniforms they once found so boring!

But things started to change as Cynthia began to pay a bit more attention to politics. When she was a student at Our Lady of Grace, she never heard much about politics. Being Catholic meant loving God and being nice to others, and "being nice" was always communicated in a personal way, but it was never translated into political action, like contributing to the common good. Taking care of the poor was discussed lots, especially during Lent and Advent, but it never went to the level of public policy.

The same was true of her family. Actually, Cynthia's parents were very active in political discussions and would occasionally write letters to politicians or contribute $10 to a candidate. They'd talk about this with Cynthia and her sisters, too. Cynthia's father was an active union member and would support other unions when they would go on strike; sometimes he'd stop by to quickly encourage them with words and a box of doughnuts, and other times he would spend an afternoon picketing with them. He was also active in the pro-life cause, sending $100 each Christmas to the local crisis pregnancy shelter. Her mom was more concerned with immigration. She knew how hard it was for people in some regions of the world to support a family; it just seemed impossible for those in poverty or experiencing governmental instability to provide a future for their children. She would send checks to a local immigration-advocacy organization. But, like the school, her parents did not really offer a language that connected their faith to their political and civic involvement.

As Cynthia entered high school and was learning more about politics, she had deeply embedded beliefs from Our Lady of Grace and her parents that the poor and vulnerable deserve special care and protection, both from everyday citizens and the government. But she thought these were just "nice people" saying and doing "nice things." She never got any signal that her teachers' or her parents' commitments were animated by Catholicism. So when she started to learn more about the two main political parties and the ways that neither cared for the unborn, migrants, and unions in the way she did, she decided not to register with a party when she turned eighteen. She figured that the next election was nineteen months away, and she would have lots of time to think through those three issues and cast a confident ballot.

However, things did not work out that way. And Cynthia's relationship to her faith started to become an obstacle to her ability to politically care for others more than it helped. She knew that the church cared for unborn life; this came up a few times in her schooling and in conversations with her dad, and she also saw it in the media (oftentimes portraying the church as an evil, but she brushed that off). But she never knew that the church was also pro-union (formally since 1891) and pro-migrant, with the bishops speaking in a unified voice for migrants. She, like many her age, also had a growing concern for the environment. This was quickly becoming "her" issue that she'd bring to family dinner conversations when these turned to politics. But as much as she learned and read and advocated, she never heard from her parents or the leader of her university's Newman Center or her priest that the Catholic Church's theology of integral ecology was leading the climate change conversation in interfaith circles. She didn't even know *Laudato Si'*—Pope Francis's 2015 encyclical on caring for creation and one another—existed. She was disappointed that, as far as she knew, the church was silent on such a critical issue. She began to get more and more involved in her campus's environmental advocacy group and told them she'd help out all weekend for a big "get out the vote" door-knocking effort to educate residents on an important measure.

Cynthia, for the first time ever, *chose* not to go to Mass that week. It was a difficult hour for her; she knew she was supposed to be at church. But after that, missing Mass was not as big of a deal. She'd go to her home parish with her family when she was back in town for holidays, and then she enjoyed the familiar faces and songs, but she went from weekly Sunday attendance to attending monthly at the Newman Center. She still went for the food and fellowship just about weekly at the Tuesday "Dollar Dinner," but knew Tuesday Mass did not "make up" for missing Sundays. When one of the core team students asked if everything was okay, she just smiled and nodded, "I'm just really busy with classes and work." If she were honest, she would have said that the homilies weren't telling her anything she didn't already know—God loves you, be a good person, cultivate prayer—and, really, they weren't telling her enough. The problems of this world are big, she might have said, and why is the church not seeing that? And all the "being nice" that she was told and shown, in ways big and small—what did any of it matter or mean? Yes, the church is a voice for the unborn and does beautiful things for impoverished communities everywhere, but what about migrants, laborers, the climate, victims of racism, and all the others who are excluded and forgotten?

Cynthia graduated and moved closer to home, about an hour drive. It was close enough that she *could* go home on weekends—and when she did, she'd always attend Our Lady of Grace with her family—but more often she stayed in her new area. She rarely attended Mass at her new parish, St. Monica's, but never failed to on Ash Wednesday and Palm Sunday. Cynthia thinks the church is good for some people, but is largely irrelevant for her.

As she looks out the window at the leaves clinging to the branches, she wonders how long she'll hang on for. Advent is coming. She has a longing for the beauty of the season, but still feels a dissonance, like it's "all eyes on heaven" when she also cares about the here and now. She recalls Decembers with deep fondness: waking early and gathering in the predawn cold with songs and hot cocoa for Las Mañanitas, the increasingly shorter days outside that were met with the increasing brightness of the Advent wreath, Las Posadas, nativity plays, Christmas Eve parties that spilled into Christmas morning . . . she's just not sure what to make of all this anymore.

Cynthia represents one type of cultural Catholic: the type who slowly drifts away because they do not see how their progressive political commitments can be reconciled with their faith. For readers who know Catholic social teaching, it is tragic that Cynthia is not aware of how deeply committed the church is to many—what we call in the United States—"progressive" causes, including climate change, racial justice, immigration, anti–death penalty, ending the social causes of poverty, and many more issues that come to the aid of those who are poor or vulnerable. It is a common saying that Catholic social teaching is "one of the best kept secrets of the Catholic Church," and it is this lack of promotion that causes progressively minded Catholics—as well as progressives in other faith traditions—to leave religion altogether; they just cannot find their place in a religion that appears to only endorse politically conservative issues.[1] Further, there is a growing "God gap" in our country, where progressive thinking is expected to align with low religiosity and conservative thinking with high religiosity.[2] This can cause those who are more politically progressive to feel that their faith simply does not "fit" and must be rejected given their political commitments.

"[T]here is evident division in the episcopacy of the United States about the prominence that the abortion issue should have over all other political issues, I think that is played up very much in the press. And I think that many Catholics just equate the bishops' entire position on politics with abortion and maybe opposition to same sex marriage. I don't know how seriously they take teachings on the environment, teachings on the poor, teachings on migration."

—Bishop John Stowe, Diocese of Lexington

The quantitative data reveal that most cultural Catholics are not as active and struggling like Cynthia, but most are simply less influenced by church teaching and less civically engaged than more frequently attending Catholics. This chapter will explore the contours of cultural Catholics' political identity, including how they vote. Next, it will determine the extent to which cultural Catholics agree with the church on select political issues. It will then explore the civic behaviors of cultural Catholics. This will lead to the final piece of the chapter: a brief "excursus" that examines the role of religious belonging and virtuous living in personal and social flourishing.

Political Identity

We will begin with a broad overview of the ways cultural Catholics understand and enact their political identity. Thirteen percent of cultural Catholics identify as very liberal (compared to 6% of regular attenders), 21 percent consider themselves moderately liberal (16% of frequent attenders do so), 32 percent identify as moderate (31% of frequent attenders), 22 percent understand themselves as moderately conservative (30% of frequent attenders), and 12 percent think of themselves as very conservative (16% of regular attenders). As these data demonstrate, cultural Catholics as a whole are very symmetrically distributed along this political spectrum (34% total identify as liberal and 34% as conservative); this is not the case with regular attenders, a plurality of whom—46 percent—lean conservative.

Political Identity. "Which of the following most closely reflects your political position?" Very and moderately liberal combined. "With which political party do you generally identify?," "For whom did you vote [in the presidential election in November 2016]?," "Do you approve or disapprove of the way Donald Trump is handling his job as President?" Percent disapproving.

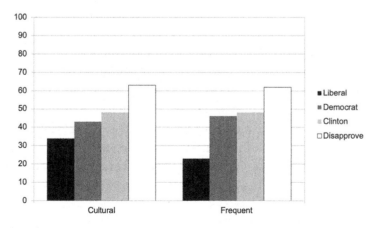

Turning next to the political affiliation of cultural Catholics, a plurality are Democrats at 43 percent (46% of frequent attenders are Democrats). Another 27 percent identify as Republican (29% of frequent attenders) and another 25 percent identify as independent or do not identify with a political party (20% of frequent Mass-goers). Although the differences are rather small, it worth noting that regular Mass attenders are more likely to identify with either party than are cultural Catholics, who are slightly more numerous among those not identifying with a party. Perhaps there is a general institutional suspicion that characterizes some cultural Catholics, creating both religious and political institutional distance.

When asked whether they voted in 2016, 74 percent of cultural Catholics said yes (compared to 79% of regular attenders). Of those who voted, 48 percent voted for Hillary Clinton (48% of frequent attenders), 43 percent voted for Donald Trump (compared to 42% of frequent attenders), and 8 percent voted for another candidate (10% of regular Mass-goers did so). We also asked the whole sample whether they approved of the job Donald Trump was doing as president. Thirty-five percent said yes (compared to 37% of regular attenders) and 63 percent said no (62% of frequent attenders). Given this fairly wide swath of political questions, cultural Catholics are very similar in their political identity compared to frequent attenders. They are more likely to identify as liberal (34% compared to 23%) and slightly less likely to have voted in the most recent presidential election. But aside from these differences, cultural Catholics and frequent Mass-goers look remarkably similar in these political areas.

Before too much can be made of Catholic voting patterns (either cultural Catholic or frequently attending Catholic), there was a final question to determine what "role [religion played] in your decision to vote for the person you did." Church leaders will be quite disappointed to learn that, for the vast majority of all Catholics, religion plays no role in discerning their voting choice. One percent of cultural Catholics voted for their presidential choice because of the candidate's religious beliefs, 2 percent voted for their candidate because of their own religious beliefs, 0 percent voted for the candidate of their pastor's or bishop's recommendation, and a full *96 percent said religious beliefs played no part in their decision.* The percentages for frequently attending Catholics are relatively more hopeful, but ultimately likely disappointing for church leaders, at 8 percent, 18 percent, 1 percent, and 75 percent, respectively. Given the fact that so few Catholics conscientiously allow their religious beliefs to inform the way they vote, it is not entirely surprising that cultural Catholics and those who attend frequently look so similar to one another. These findings all taken together illuminate a relative messiness to public Catholicism. On the one hand, cultural Catholics are symmetrically spread across the liberal/conservative spectrum with fewer at the extremes, even while they lean Democratic. They also, like American Catholics as a whole, do not have a strong sense of their political commitments as being connected to their faith. On the other hand, much ink has been spilled on an experience of division or polarization among Catholics.[3] This both/and reality of Catholicism and politics is a challenge for pastoral leaders and raises many questions for further study.

Church Teaching on Political Issues

Cultural Catholics were asked the extent to which the position of the U.S. bishops affects their own thinking on an issue. They had three possible responses that best described how they engage official teaching: 1) "The bishops' views are irrelevant to my thinking about politics and public policy"; 2) "I consider what the bishops have to say, but ultimately make up my own mind"; and 3) "I try to follow the bishops' guidance and instructions on political and public policy matters." Fifty percent say they consider the positions of the U.S. bishops in formulating their personal opinions on these topics (compared to 60% of frequent attenders) and 47 percent see the official teaching as irrelevant (compared to 25% of frequent attenders); only 3 percent say that they try to follow the bishops' guidance on political matters (compared to 15% of frequent attenders). If we combine the 50 percent group with the 3 percent group, it becomes apparent that only a small majority of cultural Catholics consider the bishops' position when discerning political matters. For the glass half-full reader, this may be heartening at first. But when simultaneously considering that cultural Catholics rarely attend Mass, it raises the question as to whether they actually know the bishops' position on any of these issues, especially in light of the previous chapter revealing that only a handful of cultural Catholics—12 percent or less, depending on the resource—consult Catholic resources when they face a moral decision.

"In some ways, the most countercultural thing the church teaches is not that all life's sacred or that the poor ought to come first or war is the last resort. It's that politics is a good thing and participation is an obligation."

—John Carr, Founder, Georgetown University's Initiative on Catholic Social Thought and Public Life

Although few cultural Catholics say they take religious beliefs into account when discerning church teaching, it is still important to explore the content of their beliefs and to see the extent to which their beliefs align with or depart from official Catholic positions. We asked Catholics to weigh in on three issues that the USCCB has taken clear stances on and even informed them whether the bishops support or oppose each position. It may not initially be surprising that regularly attending Catholics have a higher rate of agreement with the bishops on political issues. But it is striking that even though more regularly attending Catholics identify as conservative, their agreement with Catholic teaching persists even for issues that align with the Democratic Party platform! Sixty-nine percent of cultural Catholics agree with the USCCB's position on health insurance (compared to 73% of frequent attenders), 65 percent (compared to 78%) agree with making immigration easier for families, and less than half—44 percent—agree with the bishops' opposition to the death penalty (compared to 60% of regular attenders). Although the difference in responses for the health insurance question is slight, it is quite dramatic for the immigration and death penalty questions.

Agreement with Bishops on Immigration, Health Care and the Death Penalty. "Please indicate whether you strongly agree, somewhat agree, somewhat disagree, or strongly disagree with the American bishops on each of the following issues: Support for expanding government-funded health insurance, opposition to the death penalty, support for making the immigration process easier for families" ("Strongly" and "Somewhat agree" combined):

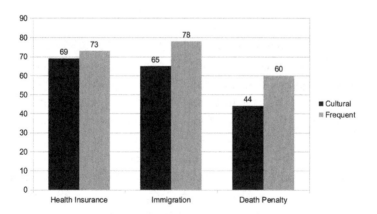

There are a few perspectives with which to approach these findings. First, roughly two-thirds or more of cultural Catholics agree with their bishops on two of these three issues; this is an optimistic read, perhaps a belief that even with their loose tethering to institutional Catholicism, they still have a distinctly Catholic way of viewing the world, sometimes referred to as a "Catholic imagination."[4] Second, there is the more pessimistic realization that over half of cultural Catholics, even with a more liberal self-identification than frequent attenders, disagree with the USCCB's opposition to the death penalty. Third, although ideology and party identification demonstrate much political similarity between cultural Catholics and frequent Mass-goers, these findings in relative agreement with the USCCB on specific issues distinguish cultural Catholics from frequent attenders on specific political attitudes.

"Catholics should not be comfortable with either party. Because certainly I think the Republicans are great on the abortion issue but they're not so great on the immigration issue or the health care issue."

—Dan Misleh, Founder, Catholic Climate Covenant

Recalling the more "Republican-friendly" issues that were discussed in previous chapters, 77 percent of cultural Catholics claimed a person could be a good Catholic without obeying the church's teachings against abortion and 84 percent believe that someone can be a good Catholic without obeying the church hierarchy's opposition to same-sex relationships; the corresponding percentages for Mass-attending Catholics are 50 percent and 63 percent, respectively. It is not that cultural Catholics are more liberal or more conservative than frequent Mass-goers. Instead, it appears that Mass-attending Catholics are simply more likely to agree with the church's teaching, regardless of whether it is on a Republican- or Democrat-friendly issue. The tug of church teaching on the issue is either weaker or nonexistent among cultural Catholics compared to frequent Mass attenders.

Civil Society and Civic Engagement

There is much discussion as to whether the United States is becoming more religiously or secularly influenced. As far as the perception among cultural Catholics goes, 8 percent say that religion is increasing its influence on American life, the majority—56 percent—say that it is losing its influence, and 36 percent say that it is about the same as always. More frequent attenders are about twice as likely to say they see an increasing influence of religion on American life at 15 percent, with a slight majority—51 percent—seeing a decrease, and 34 percent perceiving little to no change. When asked about the influence of Catholicism specifically on American life, the numbers were similar, albeit with slightly less influence. Five percent of cultural Catholics believe Catholicism is increasing its influence on American life, 54 percent believe Catholicism's influence is decreasing, and 41 percent say that this is about the same as always. These figures are 14 percent, 48 percent, and 39 percent, respectively, for more frequently attending Catholics.

Although the aggregate political identity of American Catholics is very similar regardless of whether one is frequently or infrequently attending, and there is a more substantial gap between these groups on the Democrat-aligned issues, with an increasing gap on Republican-aligned issues, nowhere is this gap more pronounced than in their actual behaviors. With the exception of volunteering in their community, the percentage of cultural Catholics participating in these activities—from financial donations to volunteering with low-income populations—is less than half of those who are regular attenders. It is quite easy to hold an attitude or belief; rarely do our beliefs cost us anything, especially if they are kept private. However, when people are willing to part with money or time to support a cause, this signals that these are much larger commitments and, probably, a more significant part of their identity.

Turning to the percentages of cultural Catholics who report engaging in these activities "regularly" or "occasionally," 35 percent of cultural Catholics volunteer in their community, 31 percent donate to their parish, 29 percent donate to Catholic organizations or causes, 24 percent volunteer to help poor or otherwise vulnerable groups, 17 percent participate in ecumenical or interfaith gatherings, and 15 percent are involved in their parish beyond attending Mass. A few things jump out just looking at these numbers. First, although it is difficult to discern how frequent "regularly" or "occasionally" means to respondents, 15 percent (about one in seven) of cultural Catholics—who by definition infrequently attend Mass—still are involved in their parish *aside from attending Mass* regularly or occasionally. This means that there is some sort of parish experience that draws a handful of these more loosely connected Catholics. Second and similarly, 17 percent have an ecumenical or interfaith community they participate in semi-regularly. About one-third of cultural Catholics volunteer in their community and donate to their parish semi-regularly.

"Citizenship for us Catholics should really revolve around our recognition that the common good should be primary. And our private interests—whether those private interests are partisan or business interests and so forth—that those things should be secondary. The common good should come first. And we should recognize that because of the primacy of the common good, our citizenship should be based primarily on solidarity—the solidarity that we feel among ourselves as part of a community with an almost corporate sense of community. And American individualism and American competitiveness and so forth, make that that hard. But ideally that's what our citizenship should be. And so we should participate for the common good. We should engage in public life in solidarity with other citizens."

—Dr. Stephen Schneck, Founder and Director,
Catholic University of America's Institute
for Policy Research and Catholic Studies

Civic Engagement. "In the past six months, how often have you engaged in the following activities? Volunteering in my community, giving financial contributions to my parish, financial contributions to Catholic organizations or causes, doing voluntary work with poor people or other vulnerable groups in society, engaging in interfaith or ecumenical gatherings, being involved in my parish beyond attending Mass?" ("Regularly" and "Occasionally" combined):

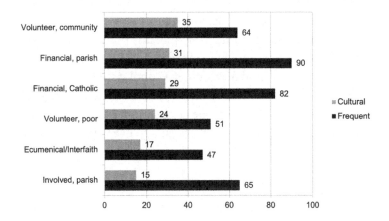

Looking at the differences between cultural Catholics and those who attend monthly or more frequently, again, the differences are vast. For some, it is fair to say that this is expected; those who attend Mass regularly would be more frequent donors to their parish and other Catholic causes, and more frequently attend interfaith or parish activities. But the fact that they are so much more likely to volunteer in their community and with poor or vulnerable groups is not obviously connected to religiosity. Or is it? As will be discussed below, prosocial practices are more likely to be found among religious Americans than among nonreligious Americans. Given this, it is worth having a bit of an excursus here on the secular or humanitarian case for religion.

Of course, for believers, religion is about participating in a life that connects them to the divine. For Catholics, this happens

through individual and communal prayer, Scripture study, theological reflection on everyday life, the sacraments, service to the
least of these, contemplating the communion of saints, pilgrimage and retreat, and the like. However, beyond explicitly religious
motivations (i.e., to worship the living God) and indirect benefits (e.g., wisdom, forgiveness, grace . . . usually summarized as
"holiness"), there are also human benefits. There are a variety of
studies that document these benefits of religion and living according to the virtues (e.g., love, generosity, gratitude) for the self and
society in human terms (e.g., lower stress levels, greater levels of
happiness). If you are wondering how this excursus connects to
cultural Catholics, it is because religious living is not just a duty or
responsibility, it is good news. When Catholicism is practiced as a
core piece of a healthy and whole person's identity, it is life-giving
to the person as well as everyone he or she encounters. If you ever
needed a justification as to *why* you should live your faith joyfully
and *why* you should not feel preachy or pietistic when you see the
chance to share your faith, this brief excursus shows that religious
belonging and virtue-based living, both of which are foundational
to Catholicism, are the keys to human flourishing. Hopefully, by
the end of this, I will have presented a compelling enough story
that you will feel wrong *not* to share your faith!

An Excursus on Human Flourishing and Religion as a Personal and Social Good

This section does not provide an argument for the *theological*
justification for religion, which for believers is the primary, if not
exclusive, reason for believing and practicing their faith; much
has been written on this throughout the course of Christian history, and I defer to these sources. Instead, this section offers an
argument for the *human* justification for religion, that is, the ways
religious belonging and virtuous living contribute to personal and
social flourishing. Please note that religious belonging (i.e., belonging to a place of worship in which adherents regularly gather for

prayer) and virtue-based living are not exclusive to Catholicism, and virtuous living is not exclusive to religion broadly. However, my primary focus will be on Catholicism, and I will also bring in sources beyond this tradition, too, as appropriate.

Pope Francis's *Evangelii Gaudium* (The Joy of the Gospel) came out of the Pope Benedict–led XIII Ordinary General Assembly of the Synod of Bishops (2012), in which they discussed the theme "The New Evangelization for the Transmission of the Christian Faith." I consider this apostolic exhortation to be a foundational document in understanding the active Catholic's role in sharing the faith with others. There are three "settings" in which this new evangelization takes place. The first is ordinary pastoral ministry, which is directed toward the faithful so that they might deepen their spirituality and better respond to God's love in their lives. Important for our purposes, this first setting includes both those who engage in regular worship as well as those "*who preserve a deep and sincere faith, expressing it in different ways, but seldom taking part in worship.*"[5] The second setting is for "*the baptized whose lives do not reflect the demands of Baptism*"; as this analysis reveals, cultural Catholics might come from either of these areas. The third setting is for those who are not connected to or who reject Christ. As everyone in this sample identified as Catholic without prompting, it appears that these first two settings are most appropriate for thinking about ways to evangelize cultural Catholics. The specifics of these pastoral plans will be discussed later in this volume. Again, this section will briefly explore some of the sociological reasons—communal and personal benefits—that may convince some readers that they are doing people a tremendous favor when they invite them into life with God and the virtues.

A good number of sociologists and psychologists who study virtues—like gratitude, hope, and compassion—find that there is a tremendous benefit to practicing these. For instance, experimental subjects who engage in daily gratitude reflection end up getting more physical exercise, have higher relationship satisfaction, and have fewer symptoms of illness.[6] Connecting this to the social value of evangelization, religions have tended to be the social vehicle in which virtues are cultivated.

In *American Grace*, sociologists Robert Putnam and David Campbell report the findings from their 2006 and 2007 Faith Matters Surveys.[7] They explore religion's prosocial role in depth in their chapter "Religion and Good Neighborliness." They find that, with the exception of religious Americans being less tolerant than nonreligious Americans, religious Americans are more engaged and simply "nicer" than those who are not. The authors created a religiosity index with the following six questions: 1) How frequently do you attend religious services? 2) How frequently do you pray outside of religious services? 3) How important is religion in your daily life? 4) How important is your religion to your sense of who you are? 5) Are you a strong believer in your religion? 6) How strong is your belief in God? With this combination of objective and subjective, personal and communal questions, they were able to place participants along a religiosity scale and compare them to others.

Turning to some of their findings, we see that religious people are more generous with their time. Of all people who volunteer for a religious group, 91 percent volunteer for at least one secular group; of those who did not volunteer for a religious group, 69 percent did not volunteer for a secular cause, either. Further, of the quintile of their sample that was the lowest in religiosity—that is, the 20 percent of their sample that was least religious—5 percent had volunteered with a religious group in the last twelve months and 42 percent had volunteered with a secular group; the corresponding figures for the highest religiosity quintile are 60 and 61 percent, respectively. Expressing this in a more tangible way, the average weekly churchgoer volunteers an extra 10.5 hours per month with religious groups and an extra 6.4 hours with secular groups than the average yearly churchgoer!

Putnam and Campbell also analyze the data from the General Social Survey, a nationally representative survey conducted every two years. This survey asked participants about 15 good deeds they may have performed in the last twelve months. Frequent churchgoers are more likely to give money to a charity, volunteer at a charity, give money to a homeless person, give extra change to a shop clerk, donate blood, help someone beyond their household with chores, spend time with someone who is "a bit down," allow a stranger to cut in front of them, offer a seat to a stranger, or help someone find a job. Five good deeds saw no difference: looking after a plant or pet while owners are away, carrying a stranger's belongings, giving directions to a stranger, letting someone borrow an item of value, and lending money to another person. No deeds were more likely to be performed by those who did not attend church regularly. Looking at these items, we see that many—but not all—of the deeds that churchgoers are more likely to perform are those that require initiative on the part of the giver. All of the deeds in which there is no difference, we can imagine that the initiation might come from the person in need (e.g., a neighbor is leaving town, so they ask their friend to watch their dog). This may indicate that religious people are more likely to seek out ways to initiate generosity.

Religious people are also more generous with their money. Of the least religious quintile of the sample, 32 percent said that they had made no charitable donations in the last year; only 6 percent of the most religious quintile reported this. The least religious quintile reported an average of $1,000 in household giving (1.5% of their income on average) and the most religious quintile gave about $3,000 (averaging 7% of their household income). Similar to the giving of their time, religious Americans donate more money to both religious and secular causes than nonreligious Americans. They give more to nearly every cause, but stand out most in comparison to secular Americans on issues of education, youth, the needy, and international causes. All other things being equal, the odds that an American who never attends church will give money to the American Cancer Society, the Boy or Girl Scouts, or the arts is 60 percent, whereas this jumps to 81 percent of those who attend religious services weekly. As Putnam and Campbell looked more closely at their data, they realized that it was the strength of religiosity that was most likely to predict generosity more so than the particular tradition a person belonged to.

Putnam and Campbell's dataset also revealed that religious Americans were more civically active than their nonreligious counterparts. They are more likely to belong to community organizations of all types, from youth serving organizations (e.g., as a Scout leader) to being in a bowling league or a service organization (e.g., Rotary Club). The most religious quintile of Americans belong to 34 percent more organizations than the most secular quintile, and they attended twice as many meetings (six compared to three). Of the most religious quintile, 29 percent had served as the officer for an organization compared to 14 percent for the least religious quintile. They are more likely to take part in local civic and political life, with religious Americans attending on average six public meetings at which local affairs were discussed, compared to two meetings for secular Americans. Fifty-six percent of religious Americans "vote in all or most local elections" compared to 46 percent of secular Americans (unlike other measures discussed here, which show a gradual decline in participation as religiosity decreases, voting offers a U-shaped pattern, with both religiosity extremes showing more participation than the middle, yet religiosity still yields more votes than secularity).

It is not just charitable efforts, but also activism and support of other social and political reforms, that are more common among religious Americans. Twenty percent of the most religious quintile say they are a member of an organization that "took any local action for social or political reform in the last twelve months" compared to 11 percent in the least religious quintile. Unfortunately, Putnam and Campbell do not break down the following into quintiles, but they report that less than 10 percent of all Americans took part in a protest or demonstration in the last twelve months, and they do say that religious Americans are significantly more likely to do this than secular Americans. They also note that, contrary to what might be most expected given how much media attention abortion and same-sex marriage receive, more activism comes from religious liberals than religious conservatives (but the gap in activism is greater between religious and secular progressives than it is among religious and secular conservatives).

A final measure examined by Putnam and Campbell is trust. They find that religious Americans are more trusting and, perhaps, more trustworthy than secular Americans. Religious Americans are more likely to condemn a variety of behaviors—divorce, gambling, watching movies with violence, profanity, sexuality, homosexual acts, premarital sex, and tax evasion—than are secular Americans. This demonstrates the lack of tolerance alluded to earlier, but also indicates religious Americans' moral aversion to behaviors that some consider immoral. Religious people are also more trusting of others than secular people, according to self-reports.

Putnam and Campbell devote a good portion of the chapter to explaining why we see this difference between religious and secular Americans. They begin their analysis by noting that religion itself matters. Because they surveyed the same group of people at two different points in time, they can compare changes. If people moved from lower religiosity to higher religiosity, they found increased giving, volunteering, and civic engagement. If they moved from higher to lower religiosity, they saw a decrease in generous behaviors. But even assenting to the idea that religion matters for pro-social behavior, what is the root mechanism that causes this change?

The authors begin by exploring the role of religious values and beliefs in shaping religious Americans' behaviors and attitudes. They find that religious Americans are higher in empathy and altruistic values than secular Americans. Beginning with altruism, only 26 percent of the highest quintile of religious Americans agree that "These days people need to look after themselves and not overly worry about others" compared to 48 percent of the lowest religiosity quintile; religious Americans have a greater sense of being responsible for others than secular Americans do. Empathy is also correlated, with 32 percent of those in the highest quintile responding "always" as to whether they are "quite touched by the things that they see happen" compared to 20 percent in the lowest quintile. But empathy and altruism alone do not explain the secular-religious gap in generosity; when comparing two people with the same score, the more religious person engages in more good deeds. And, further, it appears that of all the questions that comprise this religiosity index (and others connected to religious belief and participation not included in the index), frequency of church attendance is most highly correlated with these various measures of good neighborliness. Social trust is further amplified by two questions on the nature of God, with those who "very often" feel God's love and "never" feel God's judgement expressing the highest degree of social trust.

Putnam and Campbell argue that the most causal power lies in religious social networks. Having close friends at church, having religious conversations frequently with friends and family, and belonging to small church groups are the most important predictors of the prosocial behaviors and attitudes they tracked. So powerful are these networks that they account for most of the effects of church attendance! In fact, their findings suggest that even an atheist who happened to get involved in the social life of a congregation (via a spouse or parent, for instance) is much more likely to volunteer at a homeless shelter than someone who is a fervent believer but only prays in the solitude of their home. They argue that it is religious belonging that matters for neighborliness, not belief. Keep this key finding—that belonging is more important than believing for prosocial behavior—in mind as we discuss pastoral takeaways later. While this correlation cannot be proven as causal, similar to increases and decreases in personal religiosity, we see that as people become more or less embedded in religious networks over the two surveys, their good neighborliness changes accordingly. Again, it was not gaining or losing friends in general that made a difference in good neighborliness, nor was it ultimately connected to the religiosity index; what made the difference was gaining or losing religious friendships. Belonging to a tradition via social networks (e.g., extended family, adult children, a spouse, close friends) should illuminate much as we consider cultural Catholics, who do not attend church regularly but still might have many significant relationships with people who do attend regularly.

This covers much on religion's role in social flourishing. Now we turn to the ways virtuous living brings about personal flourishing. St. Thomas Aquinas points to Aristotle as his key philosopher in formulating the virtue ethics tradition that Catholicism now rests upon.[8] Aristotle discusses the role of *eudaimonia*, or happiness, in ethical life. All good human action points us toward our happiness. Happiness in this context does not equate to pleasure, although it could include this. Eudaimonic happiness might be more akin to "a life well lived." There is joy, there is suffering, there are triumphs and losses. The more deeply we adopt a eudaimonic approach to life, the more intensely we experience the love as well as the heartache. This is the sort of happiness that Jesus promises in the Beatitudes in the fifth chapter of Matthew's gospel, as in, for example, "Happy are the meek, for they shall inherit the earth."[9] It is not a happiness that is free of suffering. But it is a happiness that is real, generative, authentic, and draws us closer to one another and God. It gives us life and sets us free. To put happiness in eucharistic terms, a happy life is one that is blessed, broken, and shared. I hope these various angles to understanding happiness clarify what follows.

Putnam and Campbell close their chapter with a brief look at happiness. They explain that other social scientific studies of happiness have found that it is closely connected to life satisfaction. When people are asked about their life satisfaction, this is typically consistent with what others say about us and other physiological measurements of contentment. Other studies also report that satisfaction or happiness is connected to finances (in that finances improve happiness if you are living in poverty, but does not matter much once basic needs are attended to), health, being married, and having good friendships. Other studies have also found that religious people are happier than nonreligious people. Along these lines, Putnam and Campbell found that the difference in happiness between a non-churchgoer and a weekly attender is similar to someone who makes $10,000 per year compared to someone who makes $100,000. They also found that religious relationships have a big impact on happiness, so much so that the absence of these are felt deeply; people who attend their church regularly but have no friends there have *lower* happiness than those who don't attend church at all. It seems that diversity adds depth to our lives, as people with religious friends from multiple traditions are happier than those whose religious friendships come from one tradition. As individuals grow or wane in religiosity over time, so accordingly does their happiness.

To look at the effects of virtue on our personal flourishing in even more depth, I will be drawing on some of the findings from Christian Smith and Hilary Davidson's *The Paradox of Generosity*.[10] While there are others who study other virtues, such as gratitude or compassion, this book parallels nicely with Putnam and Campbell's chapter and helps us think through the importance of virtue in our lives and in those of the cultural Catholics we encounter. Smith and Davidson's book is based on their survey of nearly two thousand Americans as well as interviews with a subset of forty of the survey respondents.

There are three key findings in Smith and Davidson's work for our purposes. First, the more generous people are, the more they receive in the way of happiness, health, purpose in life, personal growth, and more. Second, while the authors believe causality runs both ways (practices of generosity beget fruits of well-being and vice versa), they assert these practices of generosity can enhance the happiness of the giver. Third, even in the face of the positive outcomes for oneself in practicing generosity, very few Americans do. Smith and Davidson's book empirically confirms what Catholicism and many other traditions have claimed for centuries: it is in giving to others that we find the truest actualization of our selves.

We see that generosity in a variety of domains has an influence on happiness. Beginning with financial generosity, people who give 10 percent or more of their income away are happier than those who do not; 38 percent of people who give at this rate report they are "very happy" as compared to 28 percent of those who give less. The same is true for generosity of time. Among those who had volunteered in the previous twelve months, 35 percent who had volunteered were very happy compared to 28 percent who had not. Further, those who are "very happy" average 5.8 volunteer hours per month compared to 0.6 hours among those who report that they are "very unhappy."

The authors also provided a series of ten questions that asked about relational generosity, that is, how willing people were to sacrifice and care for their various relationships (e.g., "When one of my loved ones needs my attention, I really try to slow down and give them the time and help they need"). The higher people's relational generosity, the happier they were; 39 percent of those highest in relational generosity were "very happy" compared to 21 percent of those lowest in relational generosity. Similarly, there was a set of five questions that asked about neighborly generosity (e.g., how often in the last twelve months have you watched over the house or property of friends who were away?). Fifty-two percent of those who reported the highest levels of neighborly generosity were very happy, compared to 20 percent of those who never did these deeds.

When asked whether they believed themselves to be generous in financial, voluntary, or relational capacities, those who saw themselves as among the most generous were more likely to report being very happy in each of these capacities than the least generous group. Respondents also reported how important it was to them personally to be a generous person. Forty-four percent of those who strongly agreed that this was important were very happy compared to 21 percent of those who disagreed with this.

It is not only happiness that increases with generosity, but also bodily health, purpose in life, avoiding depression, and enjoying personal growth. So as not to be redundant with statistics, Smith and Davidson found the same sorts of relationships in these areas as they did with happiness. Generous survey respondents were much more likely to report "excellent" or "very good" health and were much less likely to report fair or poor health than their ungenerous counterparts. Generous respondents were more likely to also be higher on their life-purpose scale than the ungenerous respondents. Generous people are less likely to have depressive symptoms than those who are ungenerous. Finally, generous people are more likely to have an interest in personal growth than ungenerous Americans.

The direction of causality is also worth considering. That is, do happy, healthy, purpose-filled people engage in more generous acts than unhappy, unhealthy, purposeless people? Or does generosity yield fruits of happiness, health, and purpose in the life of the giver? Smith and Davidson provide a compelling analysis that demonstrates causality runs in both ways, but they also mention some fascinating thoughts and asides here. For instance, in a national study of over 4,500 volunteers, there were no health differences on a variety of measures, from number of prescriptions taken to number of doctor visits. Still, volunteers reported subjectively enjoying better health than non-volunteers. It is as though generous people see the world through a lens of hope and gratitude that fosters resilience, making their subjective reality a bit more palatable than what might be objectively expected.

Another insight that emerged, using evidence from a number of studies, was that human happiness seems to have three major determinants. About half of a person's happiness comes from a genetically determined "set point" that is largely stable. Another 10 percent is from the circumstances of a person's life. And 40 percent comes from the choices people make, such as rejoicing in their blessings or dwelling on their hardships. This offers two takeaways. First, people have much control over a full 40 percent of their happiness; this reminds people that they have some degree of agency and accountability in their own happiness. Second, *half* of people's experience of happiness is set; very little can be done to sway this. For those who, for much of their life, have struggled with happiness, hopefully this gives them reason to be gentle with themselves as well as points them toward practices that will increase their happiness as best as they are able. For those for whom happiness comes fairly easily, hopefully this illuminates that this has much to do with a lucky roll of the genetic dice, and they can find more compassion for others for whom happiness does not come as naturally.

This brief excursus should demonstrate to you the importance of religion in American culture for social flourishing, especially the importance of religious friendships and true belonging. Further, while we took a deep dive into the virtue of generosity, virtues as a whole lead to a life of personal flourishing. Keep this in mind as we consider the pastoral implications in later chapters. For now, consider what personal, relational, and social implications these findings point to in your own life.

Concluding Questions:

- Where do your civic and political commitments lie? Do you believe these are well integrated with your faith, or are faith or politics compartmentalized from other areas of your life? To what extent do your political commitments align or conflict with those of the cultural Catholics in your life? In what ways do conversations about politics or faith provide a chance for bonding with or alienation from the cultural Catholics you know?

- What are some ways you could better learn how to connect your faith and your political commitments? What are the church documents you have read on these? What political issues could you learn more about?

- What are the civic and political issues that you care about? Could you begin a ministry at your parish that helps ameliorate this?

- Cultural Catholics look similar to frequent attenders on many of these attitudes, but show a real gap when it comes to civic involvement. Given the effects of generous living, what holds you back from sharing the Gospel with others?

- How can you offer a better religious relationship to your neighbor, godchild, coworker, child, sibling, or other important cultural Catholic in your life in a way that shows authentic care (not an attempt to convert) and true belonging?

CHAPTER THREE

Parish Life and Church Leadership

Matthew was raised in a large, Catholic family that leaned conservative. Growing up, his family attended a parish that resonated
with their own sense of Catholicism; the parish had a *Novus Ordo*
Latin Mass as well as two Masses in English that used more traditional liturgical elements, like organ music and incense. He and
his family were involved in anti-abortion protests and prayer vigils
and were very vocal in the promotion of marriage as the union
between one man and one woman. He was not "into" attending
Mass in his final year of high school, but did so without complaining. When he enrolled in a small private college, he was pretty
sporadic in his attendance, but he always strongly identified as
Catholic. His conservative political commitment remained strong
in his undergrad years and he was active in the campus chapter of
Young Republicans. After college, Matthew resumed regular Mass
attendance in his mid-twenties. He got married in his late twenties
and soon started growing his family; he and his wife raised their
children in the conservative Catholic tradition they both enjoyed
in their families of origin.

Matthew's wife, Charlotte, decided to homeschool the children
with a cooperative homeschooling moms' group at their parish.

The whole family is active in the parish, with the middle schoolers altar serving and the high schoolers in their respective youth group as well as helping out with the middle school youth group. They also go to the monthly prayer vigils outside of the Planned Parenthood and attend rallies or protests whenever issues related to same-sex marriage come up. Many in their parish hold them up as a model family in their community. Matthew tries not to let this go to his head, but he appreciates the community's affirmation of his family's faith.

Matthew's siblings stayed close by, and they have a tradition of getting all the families together for dinner the first Sunday of the month. This—in addition to smaller, informal get-togethers—has kept the siblings, their spouses, and the swarm of children all very close. Matthew is especially close to one of his nephews and two of his nieces, as he is not only their uncle but also their godfather. Despite all he has going on with work, parish life, and his own family, he makes time to take them each out on their own lunch date every month or two.

Matthew was out with his godson, Luke, at their favorite Italian restaurant. Usually things were lighthearted at these lunches, as they caught up on Luke's latest speech and debate competitions or track triumphs between bites of penne. But today Luke was on the quiet side. Maybe, Matthew reasoned, his reserve was because it was their last lunch before Luke would go off to college. He'd be quite a distance away, and he would only be seeing his family on vacations; pre-grieving would be reasonable, considering how emotionally close everyone was. Matthew asked about what courses he'd signed up for, whether he was nervous, if he knew anyone, how the phone call with his future roommate went. Luke just kept giving him brief, close-ended answers. Matthew thought maybe there was just so much on Luke's heart he couldn't articulate the "bigness" and mixed feelings he was experiencing, so he just affirmed, "Yeah, going to college, away from home for the first time is a big thing. And it's normal to not know exactly how you feel in these big transitions. I was excited, nervous, sad, curious, hopeful

. . . it's a lot all at once. But know you can call me up any time and you've got me and all your family rooting for you, praying for you. You're never going to be alone. We'll always be there for you, no matter what." Luke smiled an awkward smile and finished the last few bites of pasta. Matthew offered, "Split our usual?" Luke shook his head, "Thanks, Godfather, but I don't seem to have the room for any tiramisu today." He took his napkin from his lap, wiped his mouth, and placed it on his plate. Matthew paid the bill and they went out to the car.

Matthew was just putting his keys into the ignition when Luke decided to test his godfather's promise of always being there and—through tears—told his godfather that he was gay. In what was clearly an emotional moment, he managed to cough out, "I hope you can still love me and you can still be my godfather. I know you're Catholic, that you don't believe gay people are going to heaven, but . . ." and then sobbed too heavily to speak. Matthew had no words for Luke, but leaned across the car's console and, crying himself, hugged Luke fiercely and said that he would always love him, no matter what. He choked it out again, "Always, no matter what."

After a few more hugs and nose blows, Matthew told Luke they'd get through this and just to trust in his love and God's love. With the crescendo of emotion ebbing, they both sighed, smiled, and Matthew started the car up. Luke sighed and let out an awkward chuckle and said he was glad he told him and happy with his godfather's response. Matthew sighed back, feeling himself beginning to re-enter reality and a calmer affective state, and said he was thankful he told him. Matthew asked Luke whether he'd told his family; yes, everyone knew, and everyone could share this openly, including Matthew. When they rolled up to the house, he leaned over for one last hug. Whether it was because they wouldn't see each other again until Thanksgiving or the deeply personal moment they had just shared, their hug lingered longer than normal. When they released each other, Matthew reminded him, "I'm just a call away, Luke." Luke beamed his beautiful smile, "Thanks, Godfather!"

Once Luke disappeared into his house, Matthew's head began to spin. Charlotte's reaction was similar to Matthew's, but neither of them knew what to do as far as telling the kids. Matthew felt a dissonance when he went to Mass the next Sunday, as though he wasn't being honest. Matthew and Charlotte started doing more reading on the church's teaching on homosexuality and concluded that they agreed with it. They believed that heterosexual marriage is part of God's plan for humanity; it made sense from a natural-law perspective. Catholic teaching also made sense—in contrast to that of some of the evangelical Christians they'd talked to about this—in proclaiming that people were born with their orientation rather than choosing it; they didn't choose to be straight, after all—they just were. They also agreed with the loving, pastoral approach outlined in the bishops' documents, *Always Our Children*—wherein families are encouraged to love and accept their child—and *Ministry to Persons with a Homosexual Inclination*, which outlines pastoral possibilities for this community. They also re-read Pope Francis's *Amoris Laetitia* (The Joy of Love) and paid special attention to the parts on same-sex relationships. All this reading took them about a month. At the end, they felt better informed, but still weren't sure how to navigate or make sense of all this. Matthew and Charlotte were close to some of the families in the moms' homeschool group, so Charlotte suggested she could start by hearing what these women had to say.

Unfortunately, Charlotte didn't feel like they heard her very well. They started by stating that they felt bad she was going through this, but quickly reminded her that church teaching on homosexuality is very clear. They said it would be better if she didn't tell her children; there was no need to confuse them. Some of them encouraged her to tell Luke's parents to send him to a center that offers conversion therapy. They seemed well intentioned, but Charlotte got the impression that none of them saw Luke as their dearly beloved nephew; as far as they were concerned, he was just gay and had a sin that needed fixing. When she relayed this to Matthew, he brushed this off; they were just poorly informed.

They decided that a visit to their pastor, Fr. Tom, would better guide their discernment. That night they sent him a short email describing their situation, and he suggested they stay after the last Mass for the following Sunday and they could chat in private.

They arrived at Mass feeling hopeful. Surely this conversation with their priest would bring them a bit of peace on this issue, even if it wasn't totally resolved. Their pastor was not shy in speaking against same-sex relationships, but Matthew found it a bit odd that this was the focus of his homily when the readings had nothing to do with this. Matthew was also troubled when the more condemning pieces of the homily—for instance, that all people acting on their homosexual tendencies will go to hell unless they seek absolution and amend their life—elicited the biggest nods from the parish.

They went to the parish offices after Mass and the priest opened their meeting with prayer. He then asked then, "So did my homily help? Is everything clear?" They hesitated and Matthew offered, "Actually, we've both been studying this quite a bit and we know church teaching on both the design of marriage and accepting and loving our family. We're struggling with what to do. Right now, we haven't told the kids, but we feel like we should." Fr. Tom began shaking his head, "No, it would only confuse the children to realize they love someone who is in such a grave state of sin. You should only tell them if you have to. Like, and I pray this doesn't happen, but if this nephew decides to bring a date to Thanksgiving dinner one year, and you need to tell your kids why you aren't going and maybe you'll host another Thanksgiving for the other families who don't want to expose their children to this." The pastor continued speaking, but Matthew could not believe what he was hearing. When Matthew and his wife had researched this topic, they had also come across the testimony of a couple who spoke at the Vatican during the Synod on the Family. The couple had mentioned a family who had accepted their son's boyfriend lovingly into a Christmas gathering. Matthew and Charlotte couldn't imagine holding an alternate Thanksgiving, especially one that would alienate anyone who wanted to spend Thanksgiving with Luke. Fr. Tom's approach seemed to be informed only by church teaching on same-sex relationships, void of anything from *Amoris Laetitia, Ministry to Persons with a Homosexual Inclination,* or *Always Our Children.* Matthew could feel his head swirling. Fr. Tom seemed out of touch with what he was going through.

They continued to attend Mass and were active in nearly all the same ways; the only change was that they just did not have the same enthusiasm for halting gay marriage laws and simply avoided these efforts. Charlotte said she did not feel quite as accepted by the homeschooling group; most of her relationships stayed the same, but there were a handful of moms who seemed to cut conversations short. Soon this same sense of a lack of acceptance was felt at church. Charlotte and Matthew were asked if they could move from teaching confirmation to helping out counting the money on Sundays; they were told that it's good to get "fresh blood" in there every now and then, but they couldn't help but think that it was because word had gotten out that Matthew's godson was gay and they weren't "doing anything about it." Even one of their children's best friends—another homeschooler—stopped sleeping over. They could never say for certain whether this was related to Luke, but it all seemed to happen at the same time.

The final straw was when Matthew woke up Sunday, June 12, 2016. He checked his phone. Luke had sent him a very emotional text with a link to a news article covering the Pulse Nightclub massacre, a shooting in the gay nightclub that killed 49 people and wounded another 53. Matthew was beside himself. After a lengthy and heartfelt conversation with Luke, he headed to Mass for some consolation of his own. But Fr. Tom said nothing about the shooting. Matthew gave him the benefit of the doubt: he had also said the earlier 8:30 Mass, and maybe he hadn't heard about the shooting yet. Matthew went to the Wednesday Bible study that Fr. Tom led. Again, nothing. Matthew hoped that he was waiting until Sunday to discuss this with the whole parish. Still nothing. Matthew's pain was not healed by his church, and somehow it was even made worse by the silence. And he realized that talking to his pastor would probably exacerbate the pain. Matthew felt like an outsider in his parish. So did Charlotte.

Matthew and Charlotte—after a painful, two-year discernment—decided to leave their parish and start over somewhere new. But the other parishes had serious shortcomings as far as their own spiritual needs. They wanted bold sermons, but often found these lukewarm. They wanted vibrant, relational, catechetically driven family ministries, but typically these were reduced to arts-and-crafts playtimes; sacramental preparation seemed to be the only time that anything of substance was offered, but it seemed more like school than a formation program. The musical and liturgical aspects of the Mass were far too "low church" for them. But, despite the lack of spiritual nourishment, they still kept coming back each week. At least for a while.

Finally, their youngest graduated high school and went off to college. After a few weeks, Charlotte confessed that the only reason she'd been going to Mass was to be an example for the children. Unless Matthew insisted that she continue, she'd like to stop attending Mass when the children were away. As she said this, Matthew realized that he had also only been going to Mass for the sake of the children's faith. He sighed. This isn't where he thought he'd be. He decided to give Luke a call to see how he's been doing and find out whether he'd get to meet his new boyfriend this Thanksgiving.

Given that infrequent Mass attendance is the way this analysis defines cultural Catholics, it is no surprise that cultural Catholics are more loosely tethered to parish life than their counterparts on all measures. For instance, 38 percent of cultural Catholics are registered at their parish, compared to 84 percent of Catholics who attend monthly or more. Parenthetically, 38 percent is actually quite an impressive number considering these Catholics attend so rarely; parishes have at least contact information for nearly four in ten infrequent attenders. Among themselves, cultural Catholics have a wide breadth of parish experiences. There are some, like Matthew, whose parish experiences run deep. There are others whose relationships with their parishes have been fairly nominal for their adult (as well as perhaps childhood) lives. Whichever the case, these survey respondents have much to share regarding their experiences of parish life and opinions of church leadership. We also see that a looser parish connection results in a looser connection to the church at all levels. This chapter begins by exploring cultural Catholics' parish experiences followed by their thoughts on church leadership, then moves into their opinions on moral authority and concludes by highlighting some assets to the parish.

Parish Experiences

For U.S. Catholics, parishes are the primary point of encounter with Catholicism. For better or for worse, and in contrast with the broader institutional focus of the media, American Catholics experience and internalize Catholicism at the local level of the parish. Because of this priority of the local, parishes have the capacity to make or break a person's relationship with Catholicism. Again, as in other sections of this book, there will be differences between cultural Catholics and frequently attending Catholics. In exploring parish experiences, this section more directly confronts the "chicken-or-egg" question that runs subtly throughout the book. That is, do the differences between cultural and frequently attending Catholics reflect why cultural Catholics have decreased their attendance? Or do cultural Catholics perceive parish experiences or harbor particular beliefs because they are uninvolved in parish life? For example, did cultural Catholics find parishes too big and impersonal when they attended regularly and so now attend less frequently? Or does attending less frequently—thereby knowing few, if any, parishioners—result in experiencing a parish as less warm than those who attend more frequently do? The data cannot determine causality, and likely this runs both ways; but even without direct causal links, the findings still raise important questions for ministers and church leaders to consider.

We asked cultural Catholics about their experiences with parishes and parish leadership. In some areas they look very similar to Mass-attending Catholics. In others there are important distinctions. Cultural Catholics show considerable overlap with Mass-attending Catholics, with roughly two-thirds believing that most Catholics do not want parish leadership roles and about half agreeing that pastors do not know how to reach out to the laity to involve them in parish life. There are noticeable gaps in the other questions. While strong majorities of both groups agree that priests do a good job, there is still a 9 percent gap here. The agreement drops overall and the gap widens to 15 percent when survey participants are asked whether church leaders are out of touch with the laity, and there is a 13 percent gap when participants are asked whether parishes are too big and impersonal. It is worth noting that even while a high percentage of cultural Catholics communicate appreciation toward parish leaders, they still find these leaders out of touch and feel invisible in parish life. There are many reasons this could be, but the ethnic differences between clergy and laypeople could play a role; while just over half of Catholics are white, 81 percent of pastors are white.[1] If they are not properly trained in the customs, languages, and values of their parishioners, they could very well be missing the needs of their parishioners. Clearly, this is one among many possibilities. Considering how to communicate a sense of connection, relevance, and relationship in increasingly larger parishes with thinly spread priests and staff is a pastoral imperative in reaching cultural Catholics.

"Please indicate whether you strongly agree, somewhat agree, somewhat disagree, or strongly disagree with each of the following statements: On the whole, parish priests do a good job; most Catholics don't want to take on leadership roles in their parish; Catholic Church leaders are out of touch with the laity; most pastors don't know how to reach out to laity to get them involved in parish life; Catholic parishes are too big and impersonal" ("Strongly and "Somewhat agree" combined):

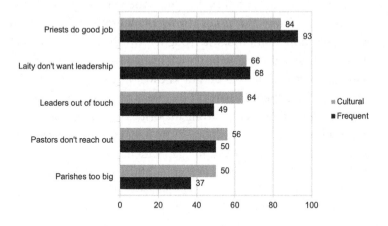

~

"I think there are some small things everybody can do . . . So many of the stories are very similar where there's these gateway moments of encounter that they have with a parish. So whether it's attending Mass for the first time to the first time you walk in the door, or approaching the parish for a sacrament, 'We want to get married here' or 'We want to baptize our child here' or 'I never received the sacrament of confirmation so I kind of want tie that one up, how do I do that?' And those moments of encounter are, more often than not, at best impersonal, at worse very detrimental and off-putting. And so the question of a parish being very institutionalized and impersonal, there are small gateway things we can do to respond to that. I always tell parishes, the most important job in the parish is not the pastor, it's the parish secretary. And if I could get my hands on every parish secretary, that would be the greatest contribution that we could make to the church. To really understand the value that when you are the first line of defense, if you're the first encounter people have—the usher holding the door when you come in for Mass, and you mess up the Mass times because their website hasn't been updated in 400 years and you came at the wrong time and that wasn't your fault! How these people respond in that moment of encounter can make the difference between someone saying, 'Oh, the parish life is just so impersonal, I don't fit in here, it's so unwelcoming,' and, 'Wow, they made me feel so seen and included, and everyone was so gracious!'"

—Nicole Perone, National Coordinator of ESTEEM,
Leadership Roundtable

Given that this book explores the beliefs and practices of Catholics who do not attend Mass frequently, perhaps one of the most important questions we asked is why they personally do not attend Mass more often. This was a question we only asked of infrequent attenders, so there are no comparisons with frequent Mass-goers. None of the responses received a majority, pointing to the wide and disparate range of reasons these Catholics have for not attending more frequently, but two rise to the top. Work or family obligations were named by a large minority of infrequent attenders (45%), as was the fact that the respondent is simply not a religious person (40%). These are two very different answers. A response of work or family carries with it an implication that these Catholics would like to attend more frequently, but other obligations crowd Mass attendance out of their schedule.

"Is there a particular reason why you don't go to Mass more often? Please indicate whether or not each of the following is an important reason you don't attend Mass more often: Work/family responsibilities; just not a religious person; I'm too busy; it's not a mortal sin to miss Mass; health reasons; inconvenient Mass schedule; sermons are poor; it's boring" (respondent could choose multiple reasons):

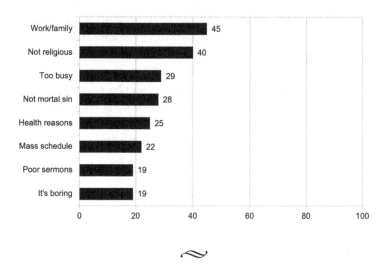

"The first three things [in the chart] tell us that it doesn't matter enough, plain and simple. Work, family. If it matters to you, you do it. Believe me, they're not missing a Green Bay Packer game on Sunday afternoon. Not a religious person? Of course they're a religious person. You just haven't hit the spot yet. Too busy, we don't even acknowledge that. You haven't hit the spot yet that says, 'Gee, I really want to be there. This is good for my life. I need this.' It's like going to the pharmacy and saying, 'I got to have my prescription refilled.' It's good for my life. That's what keeps me healthy. We haven't hit that note."

—Paul Wilkes, retired journalist,
author of *Excellent Catholic Parishes*

Understanding oneself as not a religious person is an altogether different response. Catholic teaching—as well as many secular disciplines, like sociology or psychology—assert that there are spiritual dimensions of being human. Things like a sense of meaning, a belief that one has a purpose in life, a conviction that we can glimpse something "beyond" or "bigger" when we scratch the surface of reality—all of these are connected to spiritual longings. People do not necessarily need organized religion to fulfill these needs, but these have been the traditional avenues for doing so and offer centuries-old (or older) practices—from fasting to rites of passage to contemplation to pilgrimage—to help believers become spiritually aware and integrated. The fact that so many people who identify as Catholic do not conceive of themselves as religious points to a profound failing of their Catholic experience in not pushing them to ask these existential questions. We need to not simply supply answers in formation, but to lay a foundation that includes thoughtful questions and encourages those under our pastoral care to discover how their spiritual existence connects to their everyday lives.

After this response there is a bit of a jump and then a gradual decline. Twenty-nine percent of cultural Catholics are too busy to attend Mass more often. In seeing this, it is important to understand that busyness in itself is not really an answer. When people claim to be too busy, it simply means that the commitment under question is not a priority given the other ways they have chosen to spend their time. Typically people do have time to spend exercising, playing games, reading, watching movies, hanging out with friends, or enjoying a hobby or other forms of leisure. Churches might consider two things here. First, do they demonstrate that what happens at Mass is worth people's time? That is, do they make explicit connections between worship, relationship with God, and a life well lived? Second, people deserve meaningful leisure. It was not too long ago that parishes were not simply "spiritual" places; nearly universally, they were also a place to connect socially as well as to serve the wider community and to celebrate and maintain one's ethnic identity. Some parishes continue to play one or more of these important roles. Especially in a time of increasing feelings of loneliness and decreasing social ties, parishes should consider how they might practice a more holistic model of care for those within their boundaries. This might include book clubs, community service efforts (which are also social when implemented with that in mind), talent shows, movie nights, and similar programs.

Although the obligation to attend Sunday Mass is still just as much a part of church teaching as in the past, slightly more than one-fourth say they do not attend because it is not a mortal sin to miss Mass. Twenty-five percent name health reasons; if this is the only reason people are missing Mass, eucharistic ministers should be visiting these homebound Catholics. However, although some infrequent attenders selecting this response may indeed be too frail to attend Mass, it is questionable that all are. When we parse this response out by generation, we find that older Catholics do, in fact, choose this response more often and younger Catholics choose it less often; we hear this response from 42 percent of those in the pre–Vatican II generation, 32 percent of the Vatican II respondents, 24 percent of the post–Vatican II generation, 20 percent of the Millennial respondents and 13 percent of the iGen group. While it is certain that there are people within these younger groups for whom attending Mass regularly is a real health problem, it does not seem likely that the percentages of serious illnesses or physical difficulties matches these numbers. Twenty-two percent say that a poor Mass schedule contributes to their infrequent attendance. Poor sermons and an experience of Mass as boring are each selected by 19 percent of cultural Catholics. These could very well be related, as many Catholics, both anecdotally and in data, report dissatisfaction with homilies; 32 percent of Catholics are "very satisfied" with the sermons they hear in church compared to 56 percent of Protestants.[2] Better homilies (as well as thoughtfully executed liturgy more broadly) that demonstrates the relevance of what is happening in Mass would increase engagement and decrease boredom.

There are three items we did not ask about that could explain additional reasons people do not attend Mass more frequently that are not captured here: disagreeing with church teaching, having previously experienced what might be called "church damage," and witnessing hypocrisy. Disagreeing with church teaching is a part of being Catholic. What I mean by this is that Catholicism, while it contains mysteries that cannot be fully comprehended cognitively, is a religion that develops and explains teachings in a cogent and reasonable way. Catholics are expected to engage with church teaching and ultimately make life choices with informed consciences.[3] There is room for non-assent and even dissent within Catholicism, and the U.S. bishops even spell out what prayerful dissent looks like among theologians.[4] There are studies that indicate that previous generations were better able to navigate disagreement with church teaching alongside a strong Catholic identity.[5] And a small, exploratory project indicated that disagreeing with church teaching is an important reason that teens and young adults give for leaving Catholicism.[6] Although disaffiliating is very different from maintaining a particular religious identity even while irregularly practicing collective worship as these cultural Catholics do, disagreeing with church teaching could be a common reason for both disaffiliation and distancing oneself from parish life.

Church damage is likely something readers are familiar with even if they have not phrased this idea in these particular words. Anecdotally, I have heard countless stories, directly as well as from others, about loved ones who have been treated in a way that lacks pastoral care, and that caused lasting harm to their spiritual well-being, relationship with the church, or relationship with God. I have heard of an eight-year-old girl feeling completely ashamed when a woman came up to her father and told her that her dress was too "fitted" to be worn to Mass. A Catholic high school teacher catches two students kissing in the halls during class time and tells them they are both going to hell. Awkward treatment or aggressive lectures when cohabiting couples approach a parish for marriage mean they opt to stop going to Mass after the ceremony. A Black Catholic woman walks into a parish and is told by a white usher that St. Columba's—a predominantly Black parish—is down the street; finally tired of having experiences like this literally hundreds of times, she stops attending Mass.

Hypocrisy is a final turnoff for many. Sometimes the church has control over this. The sex abuse and cover-up is a very visible form of hypocrisy that occurred very recently among high-ranking church leaders; this sort of moral failure can lose the trust of many who choose to exit the pews, temporarily or for good. But oftentimes it happens in more ordinary ways. A woman who was previously widowed at a young age has a boyfriend of two years who unexpectedly dies. She calls the parish and asks for a visit from the priest, and it takes a week for him to return the call. After a few days of phone tag, her pastoral care is entrusted to a lay minister who comes by her home and helps arrange and presides at a small memorial service for her boyfriend in the church's chapel. But the woman felt "passed" to the lay minister and was hurt by the hand off.[7] The church has virtually no control over the hypocrisy of individual lay members, but this can cause hurt that is associated with Catholicism just the same. For instance, an uncle who claims to be a devout Catholic is caught having an affair with another woman. The anger and hypocrisy at this event can turn into a general rejection of religion more broadly. Because the survey does not ask about disagreement with church teaching, negative parish experiences, or hypocrisy, it is hard to know to what extent these are reasons that some Catholics attend Mass infrequently.

Church Leadership

With the exception of Pope Francis, who enjoys high levels of approval from both infrequently and frequently attending Catholics, there are substantial gaps (12 to 15%) between cultural Catholics' and frequent attenders' satisfaction with church leadership. Although this gap seems fairly consistent in the chart at the level of "very satisfied" and "somewhat satisfied" combined, there is more to the story when we look only at those who are very satisfied, especially at the parish level (not pictured). A large minority of cultural Catholics (48%) are "very satisfied" with the leadership of Pope Francis (compared to 67% of regular attenders, a difference of 19%). Satisfaction drops quite a bit after him, and the gap shifts in important ways. Moving from the most distant leaders to the most local, few cultural Catholics (11%) are very satisfied with the USCCB (compared to 25% of regular attenders, a 14% gap). Not many more (17%) claim to be very satisfied with their local bishop (compared to 40% of frequent attenders, a 23% gap). Only 20 percent are very satisfied with their parish priest (compared to 56% of frequent attenders, a 36% gap) and even fewer (11%) are very satisfied with their parish lay leaders (which is also lower for frequent attenders at 34%, a 22% gap).

"Please indicate your level of satisfaction with the leadership of each of these: Pope Francis; the bishops of the United States; your local bishop; your parish priest; lay leaders in your parish" ("Very" and "Somewhat satisfied" combined):

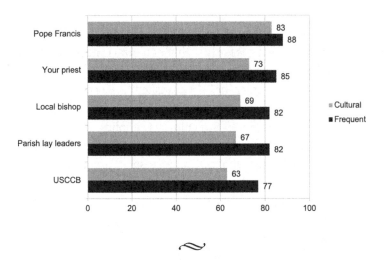

"I regularly visit with people who believe that the bishops are irrelevant because their experience of the bishops is that they're talking about issues that aren't mattering, right? And let me give you a specific example. And again, I'm speaking not from my own personal perspective, just what I hear.

The bishops just had their conference in November [2021], and you have a world community addressing a global pandemic that is killing people by the hundreds of thousands. You have poverty that's rampantly increased because of that. You have the world and the U.S. literally on fire with global climate issues. And then you have cities on fire because of the racial justice issues. And what people saw coming out, all the communications related to the bishops' conference were about whether or not Catholic politicians should be denied communion. And so for our audience, they were like, 'You [USCCB] don't have a relevant voice because you're not talking about anything that's happening here.'"

—Susie Tierney, Executive Director
of JustFaith Ministries

We can see that general satisfaction (combining "Very" and "Somewhat satisfied") is fairly high for cultural Catholics, but then drops quite a bit at the "Very satisfied" level; further, the more local the leadership, the larger the "Very satisfied" gap becomes, with the parish priest showing the largest gap between cultural Catholics and frequent attenders (20% of cultural Catholics are very satisfied with their local priest compared to 56% of frequent attenders), and the lowest percentage who are "Very satisfied" are those assessing the USCCB and their local lay leaders (both at 11%). There are a few ways of looking at these findings. First, the large gap between frequent and infrequent attenders in being very satisfied with the leadership of their parish priest is mainly due to the increased percentage of frequent attenders who are very satisfied. It is actually quite heartening that one in five people who attend Mass only a few times a year or less are this satisfied with their priest! And, as the chart indicates, when we include those who are "Somewhat satisfied," this shoots up to nearly three in four. This indicates the potential influence the parish priest may have in inviting parishioners to attend more frequently if he prioritizes personal outreach.

The low satisfaction with the USCCB points to a few explanations. First, few Catholics, even those most active, have any personal contact with the bishops as a body. Lacking this personal connection makes it hard to develop feelings of affective closeness, which points to the second explanation: negative media coverage. The most high-profile news coverage of Catholic bishops is that related to priestly sex abuse of minors and the ensuing cover-up that involved many bishops; this inexcusable response is top of mind for many. So long as their local bishop was not involved in this cover-up, there is probably a tendency to attribute a failure in leadership to the more abstract "bishops of the United States" than to their local bishop (even if they have no personal contact with him).

"We have parishes now in this church that are poorly staffed, understaffed. And so we have pastors who are between two parishes. There's no way to have that personal sense and— if they really do have that personal sense, they've worked themselves tirelessly. And then it's wonderful when you have a pastor who works tirelessly and loves it, but then it's sad when you have a pastor who works so tirelessly and grumbles about it."

—Sandra Coles-Bell, Executive Director of National Black Sisters' Conference

However, perhaps most concerning is the very low percentage of those saying they are very satisfied with their parish lay leaders. Although we cannot be certain about what comes to mind when people hear the phrase "lay leaders in your parish," we can think through the possibilities. This phrase could conjure an overly rigid employee, like a youth minister's comment that left a teen daughter feeling more judged than welcome at the pizza social when she showed up wearing a mid-thigh skirt. It may indicate a volunteer leader of a Bible study who tended to dominate the conversation rather than facilitate it. It might have been someone who was not even really a leader in the formal sense, but took it upon himself to tell the parents of a fussy baby they should take their child outside until "it" could be quiet. And even if we had rephrased the question from "lay leaders" to "paid parish staff," there is still a wide range of competence and pastoral training that lay ecclesial ministers have received. It is true that every parish priest has received his master of divinity, but very few dioceses require professional training for lay employees. Some lay ministers may have graduate degrees in theology, but most do not.[8] Lay ministers may be well versed in church teaching based off of their own study, or they may not be but still believe themselves to be; anecdotally, non-credible, partisan, or theologically biased sources on the internet seem to be catechizing Catholics more than even very accessible and reliable sources, such as Pope Francis's homilies or short videos created by the USCCB for public audiences.[9] Aside from not necessarily having proper intellectual formation, some lay ministers may not have pastoral savvy; a minister may see a teen finishing a bagel before Mass and tell her it is best for her to abstain from the Eucharist rather than to receive the host without observing the church's fasting expectations. Negative experiences that one person may consider small can have a lasting impact on the person on the receiving end that they will never see.

Although support for expanding the diaconate and priesthood to those currently excluded from these ordained ministries is strong among a majority of both frequent and infrequent Mass attenders, it is stronger among cultural Catholics. Eighty-four percent of cultural Catholics (compared to 76% of frequent attenders) would like priests who have married to be able to return to active ministry. Eighty-three percent (and 73% of frequent attenders) would like to see the permanent diaconate opened to women. Eighty-two percent of cultural Catholics (71%) support allowing married men to become priests. Lastly, 77 percent (60%) support expanding the priesthood to include women.

"Here are four statements about the priesthood. After each, please indicate whether you strongly agree, somewhat agree, somewhat disagree, or strongly disagree: It would be a good thing if priests who have married were allowed to return to active ministry; it would be a good thing if women were allowed to be ordained as permanent deacons; it would be a good thing if married men were allowed to be ordained as priests; it would be a good thing if women were allowed to be ordained as priests":

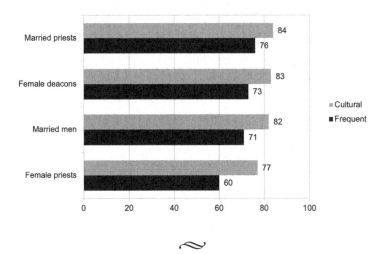

"I think people are disassociating from the church because of the patriarchy, they see that women have been struggling to find a voice and a place in this church for generations. More and more people are becoming familiar with the history of the church, especially the early Christians and the way they treated women as equals and partners in ministry and are aware of that evolution."

—Russ Petrus, Executive Director of FutureChurch

Clearly, the vast majority of Catholics in the United States support expanding the priesthood, with varying enthusiasm depending upon the group under consideration. We would be mistaken to think of this as simply a litmus test for Catholic fidelity; majorities of regular attenders are found across all four groups under consideration. I would argue instead that this gap could show that being detached from parish life causes Catholics to follow the general societal norms around inclusion and gender equality. So while the social norms may explain the greater support among cultural Catholics, it is clear that expanding ordained ministry is supported by large numbers of frequently attending Catholics as well. Conversations about some of these options are underway and may help alleviate some of the pastoral issues that Catholics currently experience, both in quantity and in quality. To speak to quantity, priests are spread quite thin right now. To have additional ordained colleagues to help with home visits, marriage preparation and presiding, spiritual counseling, baptisms, and more would be a great boon for parishes. Turning to quality, to be able to approach a married priest about a question on marital struggles or a female deacon when another woman has just experienced a miscarriage, gender discrimination, or similar issues would allow for more empathetic pastoral care. In other words, these responses may have to with a general desire to not have gender or marital status impede a candidate for ordination or, alternatively, they may reflect a desire for shared experiences and relatability in their pastoral care.

Lay Decision-Making and Moral Authority

In looking at the ways cultural Catholics would like to see more decision-making power granted to the laity, we see that they, along with frequent attenders, are strongly supportive of this. However, there are some unexpected findings in the data. First, none of these percentage gaps are greater than 10 percent (our threshold for a substantial difference). Second, even though we are working only with slight or negligible differences, cultural Catholics lead in four of the six questions while frequent Mass attenders lead in the other two. This means that we cannot attribute a greater desire for lay decision-making simply to an American democratic impulse characterizing cultural Catholics; those more connected to parish life want this as well, at times even more so than those more loosely tethered. Both questions that elicit a greater desire for lay authority for frequent attenders than for cultural Catholics are those that involve parish and diocesan finances; is it that cultural Catholics have a dip here, or is it that frequent attenders are more passionate about these areas? Probably both. Perhaps cultural Catholics, who likely give less than frequent attenders, prefer to absent themselves from this area, and frequent attenders, who have more "skin in the game," want their financial priorities to be elevated. As the chart reveals, 78 percent of cultural Catholics (73% of frequent attenders) believe the laity should have a right in selecting priests for their parish, 77 percent (83%) say this of deciding how to spend parish income, and 77 percent (74%) want this for determining parish closings. Seventy-three percent of cultural Catholics (74% of frequent Mass-goers) want the laity to have a voice in spending diocesan income, 72 percent (63%) want to help choose bishops for their diocese, and 66 percent (59%) want the laity to weigh in on women's ordination to the priesthood.

For each of the following areas of church life, please indicate whether you think the Catholic laity should have the right to participate or should not have the right to participate: Helping select priests for their parish; deciding how parish income should be spent; deciding about parish closings; deciding how diocesan income should be spent; helping select bishops for their diocese; deciding whether women should be ordained to the priesthood. (responding "Should"):

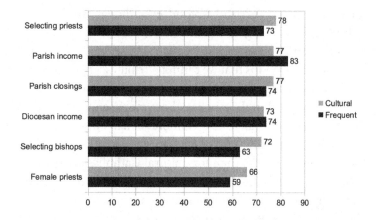

To tease out the extent to which the "lay voice" is not simply about decision-making, but also about moral authority and determining what is ethically right or wrong, we asked cultural Catholics about five issues and who should have the final say. They were able to answer "church leaders, such as the pope and bishops," "individuals taking church teachings into account and deciding for themselves," or "both individuals and leaders working together." Across all five issues, cultural Catholics are most likely (and considerably) to point to individual authority, then laity and leaders together, with leaders alone only breaking double digits with one issue (frequent Mass-attenders likewise follow this pattern on all but one of the issues, but with a less extreme individualist lean). When asked about a divorced Catholic remarrying without an annulment, 57 percent (34% of frequent attenders) said that this decision should be made by laity using church teaching and deciding for themselves, 34 percent (41%) said laity and leaders discerning together, and 10 percent (25%) say church leaders alone. When thinking about a Catholic using contraceptive birth control, they lean much harder into individuals, with 77 percent (56%) saying laypeople alone, 19 percent (29%) wanting laity and leaders to work together, and 5 percent (14%) saying leaders alone.

"We are interested in your opinion on several issues that involve the moral authority in the Catholic Church. In each case we would like to know who you think should have the final say about what is right or wrong. Is it church leaders such as the pope and bishops, individuals taking church teachings into account and deciding for themselves, or both individuals and leaders working together? A divorced Catholic remarrying without getting an annulment; a Catholic using contraceptive birth control; a Catholic who is considering having an abortion; a Catholic who engages in gay or lesbian sexual relations; sexual relations outside of marriage":

		Cultural Catholics	Frequent Attenders
Divorced Catholic remarrying without annulment	Church leaders	10	25
	Individuals	57	34
	Both	34	41
Catholic using contraceptive birth control	Church leaders	5	14
	Individuals	77	56
	Both	19	29
Catholic considering having an abortion	Church leaders	6	21
	Individuals	67	40
	Both	27	39
Catholic who engages in gay or lesbian sexual relations	Church leaders	8	19
	Individuals	68	46
	Both	24	34
Sexual relations outside of marriage	Church leaders	7	21
	Individuals	68	47
	Both	25	32

When it comes to a Catholic considering having an abortion, 67 percent (40%) say it is up to the individual alone, 27 percent (39%) say laity and leaders together, and six percent (21%) think this should be solely up to church leaders. In thinking about a Catholic who engages in gay or lesbian sexual relations, 68 percent (46%) say this should be up to individuals thinking about church teaching on their own, 24 percent (34%) say leaders and laity thinking together, and 8 percent (19%) say leaders alone. Finally, when considering nonmarital sex, 68 percent (47%) say this is up to the individuals, 25 percent (32%) say laity and leaders working together, and 7 percent (21%) say leaders alone. Clearly, most cultural Catholics privilege an individualist locus of moral authority, and very few say that church leaders hold sole authority over these matters. However, our survey option for "individuals" assumes that these individuals are making these choices using church teaching (see question phrasing); it is impossible to say how many of these respondents believe that Catholics must make decisions that engage church teaching (as the question states) or if they would have preferred a response that left discernment entirely to the individual (and did not require engagement with church teaching).

The Importance of the Parish

Although these findings on parish experiences are only discussed now, this belated revelation should by no means signal that the parish is a peripheral institution for Catholics (cultural or frequently attending). I argue that the parish is the most important locus for American Catholic life, and that the key to enlivening the faith of Catholics means being very intentional in how we go about parish life, from liturgical choices to relationship building to parish programming to our warmth toward one another in the pews. Even though cultural Catholics, by our definition, are only loosely tied to parish life, the parish still plays a critical role in serving their pastoral needs and, potentially, bringing them back into the pews.

Parishes are the most visible manifestation of Catholic life today. They are located in neighborhoods and city centers. They bring frequently attending Catholics together for faith formation, service opportunities, and community. Even in considering the infrequency of Mass attendance among cultural Catholics, parishes still gather them for baptisms, weddings, and other sacraments, in addition to funerals and holy days like Ash Wednesday, Easter, and Christmas. Even while Catholicism is a global faith, people associate the faith most intimately with their experiences at the local level. Given the prominence of the parish in Catholics' imagination, we need to take seriously what happens at the parish level. The good news here is that most readers can most easily effect change at the parish level, so in thinking through how each of us might personally reach out to cultural Catholics, changes and strategies at the parish level should be top of mind for all of us. Without going into ideas for pastoral practices—which will be the focus of a later chapter—I want to raise four institutional assets of parishes. At a time when parishes as an institution are actually quite weak—parish closings being the most heart wrenching and visible reminder of this[10]—we need to also recognize the positional strengths and advantages the parish has that other arms of the church do not. These assets are access, generalization and specialization, territory, and a space for encounter.

"So many young adults I encounter aren't even thinking that much about what's happening in Baltimore right now [interview took place during the November 2021 USCCB meeting], but they're thinking about the fact that they went to St. Mary's to try to get a certificate to be a godparent and didn't know where to go and people were kind of rude or whatever. So they're not thinking about church as this big thing. To your earlier question ["What does 'church' mean to you?"], church for young adults isn't this big, big entity.

Church for them is the most local and what we do in those little, local moments."

—Nicole Perone, National Coordinator
of ESTEEM, Leadership Roundtable

Beginning with access, parishes are uniquely situated to connect with cultural Catholics. First, as stated above, parish buildings are visible reminders of Catholicism. People see parishes as the church in miniature. This visibility can sometimes be a liability. For example, a parish in San Francisco's Castro district became a symbolic site of protest for those in the LGBTQ+ community; the parish, however, used this visibility to reach out to them, including through a thriving HIV/AIDS ministry. Those hostile to Catholicism rarely make their objections this public; 23 percent of Americans are averse to organized religion, and 18 percent have unfavorable views of Catholics. Despite these occasional moments of antagonism, the parish remains a salient and visible sign of a Catholic space where spiritual and human needs can be met.[11]

Aside from this visible and symbolic access, parishes might also have the readiest access to cultural Catholics. As was shared at the start of this chapter, 38 percent of cultural Catholics are registered at their parish. This means pastors have the phone numbers and addresses of nearly four in ten infrequently attending Catholics. Efforts to reach out to these Catholics, especially by the pastor himself, is an easy (although admittedly time consuming) step in helping cultural Catholics receive a warm and active invitation to parish life, rather than the "we're here when you need us" approach that many parishes currently take. Going out into our communities to encounter cultural Catholics also manifests Pope Francis's image of the church as a field hospital.

Another asset of the parish is its ability to serve both generalist and specialist needs. Too often the demise of many well-intentioned parish staffs is to try to be everything to everyone. There is definitely truth in the quote that is often attributed to James Joyce, "Catholic means 'here comes everybody,'" but that does not mean that every parish can be expected to meet every need of each person who walks through the door. Rather, parishes that execute the generalist piece well are those that implement thoughtful and reverent liturgy (recognizing that "reverent" will look different depending on the context), offer homilies that are carefully prepared and relevant to their listeners' lives (regardless of whether this is for the teen Mass, the family Mass, a migrant community, and so forth), and have parish staff and parishioners who offer warmth, welcome, and belonging to one another and those who walk through their doors. They also have opportunities (perhaps even expectations) for outreach and care for those in the parish and surrounding community (such as tutoring, employment help, clothing drives, and advocacy), prayer and faith formation (from Bible studies to devotionals to retreats to movie nights), and community building (such as coffee and donuts, parish barbecues, and community celebrations). This is not an exhaustive list of generalist activities, but it points to common needs that parishes meet and amplifies that staff and volunteers must do these well. Additionally, parishes simply must address each of these areas, otherwise they are neglecting essential pastoral needs of those under their care.

And it is likewise important to emphasize the asset of specialization that vibrant parishes also do well. Parishes that really thrive are those that are aware of the gifts and talents in their parish (staff as well as parishioners) and consider how these might meet more specific needs in the community. Maybe the parish is located near a community college that has no campus ministry staff; they also count three highly engaged adults in their early twenties as well as a professor and a staff member from the college among their parishioners. Why would they not consider starting a "college-ish" group (no need to chase off recent grads who are also looking for belonging) that would serve their spiritual, social, emotional (stress among college students is high), and human (workshops on paying off student loans) needs? But imagine that many in this very geographically mobile population leave the area, with only three or four of those in the college group remaining for their first career and the start of their family. This parish might want to start a young professionals or family ministry, but unless one of the members volunteers to head this, it may not be wise to assign the creation and ministry of this group to a paid staff person. The lay minister may have the desire, but preparing for and running these two additional ministries could end up spreading her too thin, and soon the college ministry starts to suffer (or the minister gets burned out). This is what happens when a parish tries to be all things for all people. It is a good thing for a parish—even while it lovingly welcomes anyone for sacraments, Bible studies, outreach, and other "general" parish offerings—to draw discerning boundaries around what it is and is not able to do, for the good of the ministers as well as those receiving ministries.

Ideally parishes within a deanery are in active conversation with one another as to what sorts of pastoral needs they can and cannot meet. For example, although Matthew, the cultural Catholic from this chapter's vignette, preferred "high church" liturgy, others prefer Mass in a more low church style; specialization can help all Catholics worship in a way that resonates with their own spirituality. Specialization can also address needs beyond the parishioners and encourage inter-parish cooperation. The parish with three mental health clinicians who have volunteered their services each week will, hopefully, open this to the parishes that do not have these experts. The parish with the vibrant young adult group that, admittedly, does not financially contribute much, may be modestly subsidized by the deanery. The parish with a dozen lawyers may provide free legal assistance to newly arrived Vietnamese immigrants, which in turn blossoms the parish into a hub for the Vietnamese Catholic community. For rural areas, where parishes are more geographically distant and parishioners' ability or willingness to travel is a concern, ministries that are hosted at two or more parishes on a rotating basis may find success. Importantly, specialization is *not* about excluding anyone; parish leaders must be reflexive and always contemplate whether they are passing the buck in not initiating a ministry, especially for a group on the margins. Specialization should be the way that deaneries ensure *all* needs are being met and being met well, not as a way to erect barriers between the church and God's people.

Third, we so often use the word "parish" to refer to our houses of worship that we can forget another theologically significant understanding of the parish: the parish as a territory. When we remember that the parish is not just a building but a sizable and complex place that is the responsibility of the area's Catholics, suddenly the parish building is understood as a place for worship as well as a place to nourish and form believers for mission in the wider world of the parish territory. The parish building is the place where Catholics gather, and they are then sent—both individually and collectively—into their parish territory.

That the entire parish territory—schools, businesses, families, hospitals, prisons, shelters—is the responsibility of the respective parish can be an incredibly daunting realization. Simultaneously, it can be an inspiring opportunity that enlivens and motivates Catholics to action. Parishes spend nearly all their resources on personnel, building maintenance, denominational donations, property, and more in comparison to the resources they invest in the parish territory; roughly four percent of a congregation's budget goes to assisting individuals or outside organizations.[12] Often a vision of scarce resources compels parishes to be inward facing when allocating resources. However, as parishes become more mission focused, they tend to inspire more giving of time and money from their parishioners. As we discussed previously in the case of individual virtue, parishes that look generously outward inspire members to do the same. Outreach efforts may likewise be an onramp for some cultural Catholics to re-engage with parish life.

"I go to those great parishes that I study. You just want to be there. You want to be there. Mass on Sunday or stuffing an envelope or getting the food for the poor or whatever it is. You just want to be there. It's fun, it's great. Your soul is alive. If you don't have that, people aren't going to do it. The hunger of people's lives, 'I want meaning in my life, I'm confused.' All that stuff you're saying. Like Augustine said, only God is going to fill that space. We can't go with that as an opening line, because that won't do anything, but we know that that's the case, and we have to find out how to do that."

—Paul Wilkes, retired journalist,
author of *Excellent Catholic Parishes*

The final asset of parishes is that they provide members a place of encounter. Pope Francis has given encounter or a "culture of encounter" a central place in his papacy, with his morning meditation "For a Culture of Encounter" reading, "[N]ot just seeing, but looking; not just hearing, but listening; not just passing people by, but stopping with them; not just saying 'what a shame, poor people!', but allowing yourself to be moved with compassion; 'and then to draw near, to touch and to say: "Do not weep" and to give at least a drop of life.' "[13] By "encounter," Francis typically is inviting us to encounter other persons, but given that he is rooted in the Ignatian tradition, which finds God in all things, encounter can also apply to creation, and we can find God there as well as in one another.

The parish is a place that can open our imaginations to encounter. The possibility for encounter is constant: at the grocery store, on a jog, at work, in the first waking moments of our day, as we read, while playing with our children, in our grief . . . there is no moment in which God is absent. Helping us to see God's presence in our everyday lives is one of the most important gifts parishes can give the faithful. The easiest way to begin this journey is to help parishioners encounter God in the liturgy. Through seasonally appropriate music and the changing liturgical colors, parishioners can be called into the various liturgical seasons in a way that offers them different orientations toward God, from hopeful anticipation to repentance to newness to Spirit-filled mission. The homily should offer both an encounter with the Scriptures as well as a way to bring them to bear on parishioners' daily lives. The kiss of peace reminds us that we are one family in baptism. Holy Communion is an intimate encounter with Jesus that involves not only the transformation of the bread and wine, but also the transformation of the communicant and a communion with the assembly.[14] And we conclude Mass by going forth as a community of disciples to live our faith in the world knowing that the "Eucharist commits us to the poor."[15]

As parishioners come to more readily encounter God in the Mass, they can better see God's in-breaking in the graced moments of their day, especially as they come to encounter one another and see one another as a point of grace. Parishes, because of their religious and moral dimension, are places where people are more willing to be vulnerable as they come to grow in love and trust of those in their community.[16] As parishioners are open with their own struggles and supportive of others in theirs, they grow affectively closer and feel more connection not only to these individuals,[17] but to their faith tradition as a whole.[18] In addition to encountering fellow parishioners and becoming more deeply embedded in the parish community, parishes can bring people to the parish for encounters with experiences that may be beyond their own. Parishes often offer opportunities to donate time or treasure for a variety of worthy causes, but simply naming these events or providing statistics is often not enough to motivate people to action. However, stories are a powerful device for changing or deepening people's hearts and minds on a topic.[19] So don't just collect backpacks and jackets for a family shelter; have a caseworker come in to talk about the challenges and triumphs of living, breathing individuals (not "we house four hundred families each year"). Don't just have a second collection for the crisis pregnancy shelter; have a new mom bring in her baby and talk about the life-changing support they received. The parish can be a place to encounter things beyond our immediate realities, expanding our understanding of who matters.

Again, there are some pastoral practices hinted at here, and many of them are most relevant for those already attending Mass somewhat frequently, but each of these highlights key assets parishes can enjoy that can directly impact those in attendance. And, as Paul Wilkes's quote says, if there is a parish people *want* to be at, if a parish makes souls feel alive, the word will be out on the street. I once studied a parish where there was a youth group of four hundred high schoolers; the local teens considered being a part of this youth group "cool." The same can happen for parishes. People can really *want* to be there. And this energy will ripple out into the community. The key takeaway for now is that the parish is relevant and that its assets need to be capitalized upon. The parish is, after all, the nexus between the church universal and the individual believer. What happens at the parish matters deeply for a person's experience of Catholicism writ large; even minimal contact can result in deepened relationships with Catholicism. The next chapter demonstrates this quite overtly, as there is a substantial difference between cultural Catholics who attend Mass a few times per year compared to those who attend seldom or never.

Concluding Questions:

- What are the ways that you, your parish, or other organization might inadvertently contribute to moving frequently attending Catholics into the cultural Catholic category? For instance, if cultural Catholics find parishes to be too big and impersonal, are you a Catholic who reaches out to strangers and tries to personalize the parish experience? What are the ways this data challenges you to transform parish life in ways that are more relational?

- Do you know anyone who is less engaged in the church because of dissent, church damage, or hypocrisy? Have you ever listened to them to really try to understand why they left (rather than to coax them to return)? What can their experiences teach us as individuals or our organization in building trust, clarity, and relationship with those who see things differently?

- How well does your parish do on these various reasons people do not go to Mass? How well trained are the volunteers and staff in your parish? What might ongoing formation look like for ministers? And yourself?

- As you look at these questions of moral authority—individuals, leaders only, or both leaders and laity—where do you fall? What challenges or graces does your own grounding offer cultural Catholics? And what might you learn from cultural Catholics (in this survey question or findings from other chapters)?

- In considering the assets of access, generalization and specialization, territory, and the parish as a space for encounter, which of these does your parish do well? Which are areas for improvement and what would that involve?

CHAPTER FOUR

Nuancing
Cultural Catholics

For this chapter, rather than a more in-depth encounter with a cultural Catholic who manifests the theme of the chapter, we will briefly meet three cultural Catholics who have very different ways of relating to their faith. Our first cultural Catholic is Tony. Tony is in his late thirties and has two young boys. As a third-generation Italian American, his paternal grandparents spoke Italian, but— because of a concern that he might not learn English quickly—they never taught his father the language. Still, Italian traditions remain an important part of his family's life. This includes attending the historically Italian parish where he received his sacraments when he was growing up. Although Tony was an altar boy as a child, his Mass attendance declined when he just "got busy" with life; he imagined he would start attending again once the boys were born, but with he and his wife both working full time, this simply did not seem realistic. When the youngest received his First Communion last year, the parish required that they attend Mass and parental meetings during sacramental preparation, but these seven talks he went to that year—while "fine"—did not entice him to become more deeply involved in the parish community, and he is glad to have his Sundays free again. He does, however, deeply enjoy attending Mass on Christmas Eve and Easter Sunday; there is something very sentimental about being in the church on those days, with his family dressed up, the church so beautifully decorated, and the passing of the flame between his family members at Christmas. After Christmas Eve Mass, they will go home and place the baby Jesus in the manger and say the Our Father, just as Tony did as a child, and also eat his grandmother's Feast of the Seven Fishes. After Easter Mass, they will go home to have donuts and biscotti before running out to find the eggs and candy left out by the Easter Bunny.

Abby went to Catholic school as a child and has fond memories of those days, from school festivals to comments that make her giggle (she remembered a school dance with a slow song during which Sr. Agatha nudged her and her boyfriend apart saying, "Leave room for the Holy Spirit!"). She still believes in the foundational teachings of the faith as outlined in the Nicene Creed and still uses the discernment tools she learned in her confirmation program. She stopped attending Mass regularly when she started college; it was a state school, and none of her friends attended Mass, and so she just sort of "fell" into that pattern. In fact, with the exception of when a friend gets married or has a child baptized, she does not attend Mass at all. It has probably been ten years since she last attended a Mass that was not a special occasion for a friend or family member. Although she does not attend Mass, she practices other elements of the faith. For example, she gives up something for Lent each year, she prays before dinner with her family, and she wears her departed mother's crucifix every day.

Alicia was baptized one week after she was born to her immigrant parents. They took the family to the Spanish Mass every Sunday. Being Catholic was a very important part of her upbringing and included not only attending Mass, but also volunteering to help around the church. Alicia received all her sacraments at this parish and also had a *quinceañera* as a teen. Upon starting college, she decided not to attend the Newman Center, as it did not feel natural praying in English. In her sophomore year she heard ideas that made her question her Catholicism. In a history of the Americas course, she learned that Catholicism came to Latin American countries through colonialism. She read about the ways whole cultures were wiped out and replaced with Spanish and Portuguese laws and customs. She wondered whether her ancestors chose Catholicism or if they were forced to convert. How many people were forced to abandon their own beliefs and ways of life? she wondered. The more she thought about this, the more she came to equate Catholicism in the Americas not with devotion and sacraments, but with colonialism and domination. With this frame of reference, she saw the sex scandals and the bishops' cover-up as another abuse of power. She saw the ways men filled positions of leadership in her parish, while women did much of the thankless work. Rather than seeing the male priesthood as a tradition, she saw it as reinforcing patriarchy. Although Alicia still identifies as Catholic, it is a piece of her identity that she struggles with because of her baptism and the way she was raised. She feels "trapped" in Catholicism and is bitter about this. If she gets married, she will not be getting married in the church. If she has children, they will not be baptized. She may be trapped with her past, but she can spare her future spouse and children.

So far this book has compared cultural Catholics to those who attend Mass more frequently. This chapter revisits questions from previous chapters, but with an eye to better understanding the differences among cultural Catholics, specifically those who attend Mass "a few times a year" and those who attend "seldom or never." This first group is a smaller portion of cultural Catholics, making up 42 percent of them, and those who attend Mass seldom or never comprise 58 percent of cultural Catholics. Again, cultural Catholics account for 53 percent of the total Catholic population. To compare these two groups of cultural Catholics to Catholics generally, cultural Catholics who attend a few times per year account for 22 percent of all American Catholics, whereas those who attend rarely or never represent 31 percent of all Catholics.

Rather than review all the questions that have come before, we will walk through the findings that reveal substantial differences of

10 percent or more. We may make occasional exceptions, such as when percentages are so small that differences between groups are more pronounced. For example, if one group responds at 9 percent and the other at 3 percent, while this is an *absolutely* small difference (6 percentage points) it is a *relatively* large difference (one group responds at a rate that is three times higher than the other).

Quickly looking to demographics, although there was no difference between these groups as to what age they became Catholic; whether those who became Catholic as adults went through RCIA; whether they attended Catholic school; their generation, political party, political ideology, or gender, a few other categories did reveal differences. First, those who attend a few times per year are more likely to be married to a Catholic spouse (70%) than those who attend seldom or never (52%). Catholics who attend a few times per year (58%) are more likely to be registered at their parish than those who attend seldom or never (24%). Those who attend a few times per year are slightly less likely to be white (58% attend a few times per year compared to 65% being seldom or never) and slightly more likely to be Hispanic (35% attend a few times per year compared to 29% being seldom). Finally, those who attend a few times per year are more likely to report that their highest level of education is a bachelor's degree or higher (32% attend a few times per year compared to 22% being seldom), and those who attend seldom or never are more likely to report that their highest degree is a high school diploma (39% being seldom compared to 27% attending a few times per year).

Beliefs, Identity, and Practices

In looking at what elements of the faith they might consider "essential" or "somewhat essential," nearly all of these questions reveal a substantial gap between these cultural Catholics, with a gap of ten percentage points or more on eight of these nine items: belief in Jesus's resurrection from the dead (94% of those attending a few times per year and 84% of those seldom or never attending);

charitable efforts to help the poor (90% and 76%); devotion to Mary (87% and 77%); the necessity of having a pope (85% and 71%); engaging in daily prayer (81% and 66%); participating in devotions such as eucharistic adoration or praying the rosary (75% and 58%); privately confessing to a priest (62% and 45%); and the obligation to attend Mass once per week (61% and 42%). There was no substantial difference on how essential they found having a celibate male clergy (42% and 36%).

Essential Elements of Catholicism. "As a Catholic, how essential is each of these to your vision of what it means to be Catholic? Would you say the following is or are essential to the faith, somewhat essential, or not essential at all?" ("Somewhat essential" and "Essential" combined):

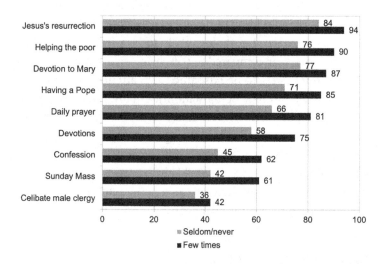

Only one of our "Strongly agree/Strongly disagree" questions demonstrated a difference, and it is important for the long-term health of the church. There was a difference when asked whether it is important that younger generations of one's family grow up as Catholics: 76 percent of those who attend Mass a few times per year agree with this, compared to 62 percent of those who attend seldom or never. It is interesting that a majority, even among those who attend seldom or never, still want future generations of their family to remain Catholic. However, to prevent leaders from falling into false optimism, it is also important to remember that these are both very large groups of American Catholics; cultural Catholics account for 53 percent of the Catholic population nationally. That one fourth of those attending a few times a year and nearly 40 percent of those who attend seldom or never do not find it important that future generations are Catholic means that large numbers of the children of these Catholics will not be raised in the faith.

There were also two standout gaps among these groups in the questions that ask about what is necessary to be a "good Catholic." These were the two items that were considered most core to Catholicism. Half of those attending Mass a few times per year say that to be a good Catholic, one must believe that the bread and wine really become the body and blood of Jesus, in comparison to 37 percent of the seldom-or-never group. The second item is about being a good Catholic without believing that Jesus physically rose from the dead, with 64 percent of those attending a few times per year saying this as well as half of those who attend seldom or never. Given that these two items are core to the sample as a whole, but that we see a substantial difference between these two groups that we do not see in the other "good Catholic" questions, this may indicate that those who attend seldom or never do not have the same facility in judging what is core, important, or peripheral to Catholicism as those who attend even a few times per year.

Another place where a substantial difference exists between these groups is the subjective importance of the Catholic Church in their lives as well as their likelihood of leaving Catholicism. The Catholic Church is not especially important to either group, but a gap remains, with 3 percent of those who attend a few times per year and 1 percent of those who attend seldom or never saying Catholicism is "the most important part of my life." Although this is only a two percent gap *absolutely*, because of the small numbers, this is a large gap *relatively*, with three times as many of those who attend a few times per year choosing this response. We see a similar relative gap in the second option, with 16 percent of those attending a few times per year and 6 percent of those attending seldom or never choosing "among the most important parts of my life." Fifty-three percent of those attending a few times per year and 33 percent of those attending seldom or never respond, "Quite important to me, but so are many other areas of my life"; this response receives the largest percentage from those attending a few times per year. Twenty-four percent of those attending a few times per year and 43 percent of those attending seldom or never choose "not terribly important to me"; this is the most popular choice for those attending seldom or never. Finally, 4 percent of those who attend Mass a few times per year and 17 percent of those attending seldom or never report "not very important to me at all"; this not only breaks the 10 percent threshold, but is also a large relative gap, with those attending seldom or never four times more likely to choose this response.

As reported earlier, cultural Catholics do not report a high likelihood of disaffiliation. When placing themselves on a 1-to-7 scale—with "1" signaling "I would never leave the Catholic Church" and "7" meaning "Yes, I might leave the Catholic Church"—the responses trend toward the lower end of the scale for both groups, but more so for those attending a few times per year. Thirty-two percent of those attending a few times per year and 23 percent of those attending Mass seldom or never selected "1." Continuing by listing those who attend Mass a few times per year first and those who attend seldom or never second, 18 percent and 17 percent chose "2," 13 percent and 9 percent responded with a "3," 17 and 21 percent said "4," 10 and 13 percent said "5," 8 and 7 percent chose "6," and another 3 and 10 percent selected "7." Because there are seven choices, none of the individual categories break the 10 percent threshold, but if we group some of these responses, differences jump out. For instance, among those who attend a few times per year, 50 percent choose "1" or "2", but this percentage is only 40 percent for those who attend seldom or never.

When discussing these numbers earlier in the book, I suggested that these cultural Catholics may be very unlikely to leave because the investment in "being Catholic" is so low for them as they attend Mass so rarely. This may explain part of the story, but in separating these groups we can see that it is more complicated than this. If it were simply a matter of "I'm sticking with Catholicism because it doesn't take much of my time or money to remain so," we would expect to see a higher likelihood of staying Catholic among those who attend Mass seldom or never. However, we see a higher likelihood of staying among those who attend Mass a few times per year. This finding makes it seem that choosing to attend Mass, even if only occasionally, also signals a deeper commitment to Catholicism. Clearly this is not the whole of the story; after all, the most popular response among those who seldom or never attend Mass was also a "1." There are many factors at play in using this likelihood-of-leaving question to better understand Catholic identity. This complexity should not be reduced to one or two factors, and it points to the need for a qualitative, open-ended interview study to better understand the ways these cultural Catholics approach their faith.

When looking at the sources these two groups of cultural Catholics use in their moral discernment, there are substantial differences in most areas. Some of these might be expected, such as the religious sources, and others are more of a surprise. There are two items that might be thought of as not explicitly religious; both still show substantial differences. Eighty-four percent of those who attend Mass a few times per year and 71 percent of those who attend seldom or never talk to a close family member. Similarly, 80 percent of those who attend Mass a few times a year and 70 percent of those who attend seldom or never say they talk to a trusted friend. The fact that those who attend Mass a few times per year are more likely to reach out to family and friends than those who attend seldom or never may corroborate other data indicating that those who are more tied to institutions are more embedded in social groups more broadly, such as that Catholics who are political independents as less tethered to Catholicism than either Catholic Democrats or Catholic Republicans.[1] The absolute or relative gap is substantial for the remaining religious items. Seventy-four percent of those who attend Mass a few times per year report they pray or meditate when facing an important decision, compared to 56 percent of those who attend seldom or never. Nineteen percent of those who attend a few times per year read the *Catechism of the Catholic Church* to aid in their discernment, compared to 7 percent of those who attend seldom or never. Eighteen percent of those attending a few times per year look at or read Catholic media for advice, compared to 7 percent of those attending seldom or never. Nearly three times as many (14%) will approach their local priest among those who attend a few times per year compared to those who attend seldom or never (5%). Nearly twice as many (13%) of those who attend a few times per year will read papal documents or encyclicals compared to those who attend seldom or never (7%). Finally, twice as many who attend Mass a few times per year (10%) go to the USCCB or their diocesan website for advice compared to those who attend seldom or never (5%).

Sources Used in Moral Discernment. "When you have an important moral decision to make, which, if any, of the following activities or sources do you usually look to for guidance?" ("Always" and "Sometimes" combined):

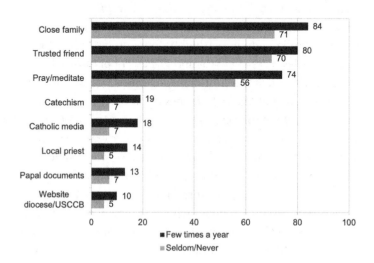

Finally, there were gaps in the frequency of prayer and confession among these two groups of cultural Catholics. Thirty-nine percent of those attending Mass a few times per year pray at least daily and 27 percent of those attending seldom or never say the same. They are roughly matched at "occasionally or sometimes" (48% of those attending a few times per year and 41% at seldom or never). There is again a wide gap with the least frequent option; 13 percent of those who attend a few times per year pray "seldom or never" as do 32 percent of those who attend Mass seldom or never. Confession is not a frequent practice for either group. Fourteen percent of those who attend Mass a few times per year meet the official Catholic expectation of confessing annually, as do 4 percent of those who attend seldom or never. Twenty-two percent of those who attend a few times per year say they confess "less than once a year," which is much higher than the 7 percent attending seldom or never who say the same. Finally, 64 percent of those who attend a few times per year say they confess "seldom or never," which is much lower than the 90 percent who attend Mass seldom or never.

Politics and Civic Life

As was mentioned in the demographics section of this chapter, there is no difference among these two groups of cultural Catholics when it comes to political party affiliation and political ideology. There is also no difference in whether they voted in the 2016 election. There were, however, substantial differences in other questions. For example, those who attend Mass a few times per year were more likely to vote for Hillary Clinton (55%) than those who attend Mass seldom or never (43%). Donald Trump was a less popular choice for those attending a few times per year (38%) then he was for those who attend seldom or never (47%). There is a similar gap when we examine approval of the way Trump was handling his presidency. Twenty-nine percent of those who attend Mass a few times per year approve of Trump's job, as do 39 percent of those who attend seldom or never. Very few Catholics—cultural or frequently attending—say that their religious beliefs influenced how they chose to cast their vote, and the gaps were very small in comparing the two groups of cultural Catholics.

Those who attend Mass a few times per year are more likely to consider the bishops' positions on political issues as well as agree with some of these, with 40 percent of those attending a few times per year saying that the bishops' views are irrelevant to their political thinking and 52 percent of those attending seldom or never saying the same. Similarly, 58 percent of those who attend a few times per year say they consider what the bishops have to say but ultimately make up their own mind, compared to 44 percent of those who attend seldom or never. Few in either group said that they try to follow the bishops' guidance; counterintuitively, this was 2 percent for those attending a few times per year and 4 percent (double) for those attending seldom or never. This very small number of those who attend seldom or never and yet still privilege the bishops' thinking on political issues (even though they do not obey the church's expectation of Sunday Mass attendance) may be among those who are totally homebound and agree with much of church teaching.

The question on their agreement with the bishops' position on expanding government-funded health insurance did not yield a difference, but the other two questions did. When it came to agreeing with the bishops' position against death penalty, those who attend Mass a few times per year (51%) were more likely to support this than those who attend seldom or never (40%). This stronger agreement is also seen in supporting the bishops' position in making the immigration process easier for families, with 71 percent of those attending a few times a year agreeing and 61 percent of those seldom or never attending Mass saying the same.

Concluding with these cultural Catholics' civic practices, the "more is more" pattern in comparing cultural Catholics with frequent attenders emerges here between those who attend a few times per year and those who attend seldom or never. That is, although it might be reasonable to expect that people who are involved in an organization or cause will commit less of their time to other organizations or causes, actually, it is more often the case that involvement is contagious and participation in one activity increases participation in others.[2] Just as we saw that frequently attending Catholics are more involved in the voluntary sector than cultural Catholics, those who attend a few times per year are more involved in both parish and non-parish activities than those who attend seldom or never.

Civic Engagement. "In the past six months, how often have you engaged in the following activities? Volunteering in my community, giving financial contributions to my parish, financial contributions to Catholic organizations or causes, doing voluntary work with poor people or other vulnerable groups in society, engaging in interfaith or ecumenical gatherings, being involved in my parish beyond attending Mass" ("Regularly" or "Occasionally" combined; other option was "Not at all"):

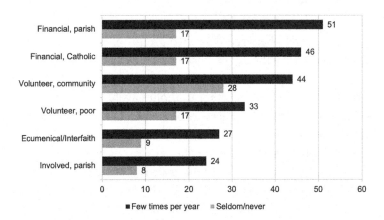

Although volunteering in non-religious contexts shows the smallest gaps, the gaps are all quite substantial. Thinking back to our excursus on generosity, even attending Mass a few times a year might make a difference in people's civic engagement. Fifty-one percent of those attending a few times per year donated to their parish regularly or occasionally within the last six months compared to 17 percent of those attending seldom or never. Forty-six percent of those who attend a few times a year donate to Catholic organizations or causes, more than the 17 percent of rarely attending Catholics. Forty-four percent of those attending a few times per year volunteer in their community, compared to 28 percent of those who attend seldom or never. One-third of those who attend a few times per year volunteer with poor or vulnerable groups, compared to 17 percent of rare attenders. Twenty-seven percent of those who go to Mass a few times per year attended interfaith or ecumenical gatherings, as did 9 percent of those attending seldom or never. Finally, roughly one-fourth of those who attend a few times per year have gotten involved in their parish beyond attending Mass, compared to 8 percent of those attending seldom or never.

Church Leadership and Parish Experiences

It is striking that for some of our questions on parish life there is much overlap between these two groups of cultural Catholics and others where the gap is substantial. For instance, there was no substantial gap on our questions that asked about whether parish priests do a good job, whether Catholics avoid parish leadership roles, whether church leaders are out of touch, whether most pastors know how to reach out to laity to get them involved in parish life, and whether Catholic parishes are too big and impersonal. They are also very similar in their approval of the pope, the bishops, and other church leaders. The gap is likewise very small when it comes to expanding what populations should be eligible for the priesthood and diaconate. There is also little difference in their attitudes on lay authority in parish and diocesan decision-making. Finally, when it comes to moral authority and whether this rests in the hands of church leaders, individuals, or both, only one question revealed a difference; 61 percent of those attending seldom or never said that a divorced Catholic getting remarried without an annulment should be handled by the individuals, whereas only 51 percent of those attending a few times per year said this.

However, there are two important differences in the reasons respondents give for not attending Mass more often. Those who attend Mass a few times per year (53%) are more likely than their rarely attending counterparts (39%) to name work or family responsibilities. This points to a desire for some to attend more often if there was a more convenient Mass time or perhaps a more family-friendly Mass experience. Those who attend seldom or never (46%) are more likely to say that they are just not a religious person than those who attend a few times per year (32%). This is a totally different concern that points to religion as something that is contrary to these people's self-understanding.

"Institutionally, I think that if I was a pastor and I saw this, then on days when I know I'm getting these people, Easter, Christmas, Ash Wednesday, I am hitting it hard how the gospel is good news for our work and for our families."

—Jason Simon, President, The Evangelical Catholic

It is somewhat surprising that there were many differences among these two types of cultural Catholics in other sections, and that this section that dives more explicitly into parish life and church leadership reveals few differences. However, an important difference they offer here is in the reason they do not attend Mass more frequently. Parishes would do well in reaching those who only attend a few times per year by focusing on the ways, as the quote by Jason Simon suggests, that participation in the faith is great for having meaningful work and family lives. And by "focusing," I don't just mean stating the ways Catholic ideas and teachings weigh in on these issues. When we have these Masses that infrequently attending Catholics are more likely to attend, we need to offer them meaningful opportunities to continue to engage parishes.

We will look more at this in the final chapter that explores pastoral ways to apply these findings in youth and young adult, parish, and diocesan and regional contexts. A quick note to the reader: Although you may work or be engaged in only one of these contexts, I would advise you to read all three sections. I have written these sections in a way that they are not redundant and will be an easily digestible "reward" for the hard work of thinking through the data in these previous chapters. So, there may be a pastoral practice in the youth and young adult section that would just as easily apply to your parish and diocesan ministries for those beyond this age demographic. I will also be using more of a conversational style and drawing upon more examples and concrete ideas. Again, I hope these shifts will make reading all these sections easier and more enjoyable and, in the end, will yield many fruits for a more effective and life-giving ministry to cultural Catholics and your community broadly.

Concluding Questions:

- This chapter opened with three short vignettes featuring three very different kinds of cultural Catholics. What sort of cultural Catholics do you know, and why do they not attend church? If you aren't sure, consider a disarming way to begin this conversation. They should feel like you are genuinely curious, not that they need to defend their reasons for not attending.

- The "Beliefs, Identity, and Practices" section revealed that there is a looser tether among those who seldom or never attend Mass. The final "Church Leadership and Parish Experiences" section also showed that those who attend seldom or never are also much more likely to say that they are simply not a religious person. Imagining that at least some of these Catholics were at least somewhat more involved in their youth, how might youth and family ministry strengthen these youth for future religiosity? How can formation teach people that they are all inherently spiritual, with deep spiritual longings?

- The "Beliefs, Identity, and Practices" section (and the moral sources used for discernment) as well as the civic engagement findings reveal that those who attend Mass seldom or never are more loosely tied to relationships and organizations broadly. What are some of the social and personal risks that might be higher for these people (e.g., loneliness, mental wellness)? How can Catholic institutions address some of these concerns of disconnect in ways that are more human and less religious, thereby meeting a need that is deeply human even for those who are uncomfortable thinking in conventional religious language?

CHAPTER FIVE

Pastoral Takeaways

Carmen is a freshman living in the dorms at a public college. She is fairly active in the Newman Center at her local college. She stopped attending Mass on a weekly basis after she was confirmed in the tenth grade, but still goes about once per month to Sunday Mass and goes every week to the "Dollar Dinner"—Mass, meal, and fellowship—at her local Newman Center. She lives in a co-ed student housing arrangement with about a dozen other students and an RA. Unlike the other dorms that are more traditional in their layout, her housemates all share a common kitchen and living room, so there are lots of opportunities to informally socialize. Two of her housemates, Randy and Paul, are Catholic, but they have not tried the Newman Center and do not attend Mass elsewhere. Carmen really enjoys the students and the priest at the Newman Center and wonders when might be a good time to invite her housemates to join her.

Not long after, at a Dollar Dinner, the student leadership team announces that they are going to have a welcome event on a Thursday evening. It will consist of a fun evening of ice breakers, fancier food, dessert, and socializing. It will not only be a student event, but the whole worshiping community of the Newman Center will also be involved; they are estimating about 250 people will attend, plus any guests they want to bring. Carmen thinks this would be a great event to introduce Randy and Paul to the Newman community.

The evening arrives and Carmen, Randy, and Paul walk across campus together. Carmen talks about what's on the evening's agenda and says that there are also really fun Dollar Dinner events each Tuesday. Randy and Paul say this sounds like an easy event to make each week. Carmen is hopeful that Randy and Paul will connect with her friends and enjoy themselves.

When they arrive about ten minutes after the start time, Carmen is really happy that there is a good turnout. Lots of people, both students and older adults and even a handful of children, have filled the parish hall. She introduces Randy and Paul to some of her friends, then heads over to the pastor. The pastor connected easily with Randy, as he knew the priest who was the chaplain at Randy's Catholic high school, and they had fun swapping stories about him. Things were going well, and Randy and Paul began to drift around the room and mingle on their own.

Then things stopped going well. Although Carmen was about fifteen feet away from them and the room was fairly loud due to all the chatting, she heard a woman in her fifties quite loudly exclaim to Paul and Randy, "I know what that means! You don't go to church! You don't go to church!" The woman seemed to be yelling this in a jesting way—she had a broad smile across her face—but both Paul and Randy were wincing at her remark. Carmen wrapped up her conversation and made her way to Paul and Randy, who had since left this woman and were talking only to each other now.

Carmen asked, "Is everything okay? What was that woman going off about?"

Randy recounted, "Yeah, I dunno. We started talking about our Catholic high school experiences and that was fine. And then how we heard about tonight and I said I was invited, that this was our first time at the Newman Center. Then she asked us where we attend church and I said, 'Actually, I'm more of a nonpracticing Catholic.' At which point she pointed at us and bellowed, 'I know what that means! You don't go to church!' And then, for good measure, she said it again, 'You don't go to church!' " Randy sighed, then continued, "I don't think this was such a good idea. I think Paul and I are gonna walk home. We'll see you later, Carmen."

This final chapter will put the previous findings in conversation with other pastoral and sociological resources, offering ways of understanding the data in light of your particular context and suggesting practices for providing meaningful pastoral outreach to cultural Catholics.[1] We will begin with some general observations and broad pastoral considerations of cultural Catholics. Next, we will discuss pastoral insights for youth and young adult contexts; while this carries an age-specific label, the ideas are applicable to those beyond youth and young adults. The third section examines the parish. The final area discusses diocesan and other regional ministries. Again, each of these areas will have insights for others, so you are strongly encouraged to read each of these sections regardless of your context.

General Observations

"I wrote an article for *USA Today* when Pope Francis first become Pope. And I talked about how important it is that people feel good about being Catholic. And how we never think about this. It was sort of beneath our Catholicism to think about. And also it's attached to hedonism and secularism and all those sorts of things to feel good. But the reality is, is that our faith should create really deep sense of feeling good. And one of the things I said was people who don't feel good about being Catholic don't evangelize. That's never going to happen. You're never going to get someone who doesn't feel good about being Catholic to evangelize. The other thing is over the last 20 years, more and more people don't feel good about being Catholic."

—Matthew Kelly, Founder, Dynamic Catholic

Very little suggested here will matter if we as Catholics are not ourselves excited about our faith. We need to know what Catholicism offers us before we try to imagine the ways it meets the longings of each person or the world. Once we have grounded ourselves in that, we will joyfully share our experiences with others. Imagine, for example, having a great meal at a restaurant, seeing a fantastic movie, or doing amazing volunteer work at a nonprofit and not sharing that with others. It just isn't done. When we have a great experience, we invite others to it. Fully appreciating what Catholicism gives us and offers to others is the starting place for evangelization. Eighty-nine percent of frequently attending Catholics want their descendants to remain Catholic compared to 62 percent of cultural Catholics. In the same way we want certain values or ethical commitments—like fairness and compassion—to be honored by our children, if we personally know what is worth passing on in Catholicism, we will want that passed to future generations.

"I think just be grateful that cultural Catholics still feel comfortable claiming Catholicism as part of their identity. Those surveys pulled up [that] people are just busy and family takes precedence. Religion back in the day was so much of the center of people's lives. Religion, these days, is on the periphery. It's not the sexy thing to look at faith or spirituality. I think how we can reach out to those cultural Catholics is really just to keep the invitation open, continually to invite them and to say, 'Hey we're thinking of you.' Not 'Thanks for still being Catholic,' but like, 'We're here. We're still here and we're ready to receive you, you're always more than welcome.' Treating it as if we are family and that when people have time then they're more than welcome to come back."

—John Michael Reyes, Director of Adult Spirituality,
St. Ignatius College Preparatory

As was noted earlier, 32 percent of cultural Catholics in our sample pray daily or more often. This is a sizable minority, but much lower than the nearly 72 percent of frequent Mass attenders who pray at this frequency. But it isn't simply the difference in the frequency of prayer that should cause us to pause. I also wonder about the quality and depth of prayer for most people who only occasionally embed themselves in a faith community. An analogy might be a person who goes to the batting cages to become a better baseball player. Of course, this person may make more bat-to-ball contact over time and improve in several ways. But if he or she never plays on a team, watches a professional game, solicits advice from more experienced players, or practices other skills like throwing and fielding, this person's ability to improve as a baseball player is going to be relatively slow and quite limited. Unpacking this analogy a bit more, what are the spiritual resources, knowledge, and wisdom that these less churched cultural Catholics bring to prayer? What are the communal stories that they can draw upon to create analogies for their own contexts? What images of God, understanding of vocation, and basic theological reflection tools are they equipped with to make moral sense of the choice before them? This is not at all to say that people cannot gather deep spiritual insights while being loosely tethered to the resources of a faith community, but that this is likely easier when believers have personal experience as well as communal resources at their disposal. All this is to say that differences in frequency or assent here are the only part of the story that this data can tell. Some cultural Catholics are missing the texture and nuance in the journey of faith that regular attenders get (admittedly to varying degrees) in frequent parish experiences. Some cultural Catholics may have much depth and theological wisdom in their spiritual life that comes from their upbringing, schooling, spiritual reading, or relationships. For others, their understanding of Catholicism may lack sophistication or be riddled with inaccuracies (which can also be said of frequent attenders, I concede!).

But the question is not, I would argue, "How do we get these cultural Catholics back in the pews?" For some, it may be. But, as

Pope Francis acknowledged in *Evangelii Gaudium* (The Joy of the Gospel), there are many who lead faithful lives even while they do not take part in regular communal worship. There is evidence that these cultural Catholics are simply doing their Catholicism differently than many leaders want them to do.[2] The missionary role of ministers and ordinary Catholics is to lead all to "respond to God's love ever more fully in their lives" and recognize the dignity of people as they discover what this might mean for them personally. There have no doubt been many pushy believers in any cultural Catholic's life (even as a weekly attender, I am too frequently proselytized by non-Catholics!); be, like Jesus, an encounter for them.

This approach of encounter connects to the final general observation. Thinking back to the reasons people gave for not attending Mass more often, 40 percent said that it was simply because they were not a religious person. This is a finding that should bring us some sadness. We have let these people down—as parents, teachers, grandparents, godparents, confirmation sponsors, neighbors, coworkers, priests, lay ministers—in not offering them experiences, questions, and conversations that reveal to themselves how deeply spiritual they actually are. When did we fail to ask the curious, open-ended question? Or when did we fail to see that a spiritual question was being asked, and we responded with a close-ended answer? Still, all is not lost. We can learn from these findings and open doors for those we encounter in our day-to-day lives.

Youth and Young Adults

Much has been written recently on teen and young adult spirituality, some of this even with a specific focus on Catholics. To highlight a few of the findings that are relevant for us, in Robert J. McCarty and John M. Vitek's *Going, Going, Gone*—a short exploratory study of fifteen disaffiliated young adult Catholics—authors found that participants left Catholicism at an average age of thirteen.[3] They said the most common reasons for leaving were that they were injured (i.e., they had negative experiences in life or with people of faith), they were drifters (i.e., they were indifferent toward religion and other activities filled their lives), or they were dissenters (i.e., they had a disagreement with doctrine). The book also recommends a "belonging-first" approach to ministry. The authors say that too often parishes take a "behaving, believing, belonging" approach to ministry, when this should be reversed. That is, rather than expecting a high school youth first to *behave* a certain way, then accept the core *beliefs*, which allows them to finally *belong* to the group, parishes should first extend radical belonging. With authentic belonging, teens (and others) will desire to learn more about the beliefs of their peer group and likely adopt behaviors that reflect those beliefs.

"I remember when I was first ordained and I came back, having studied in Rome and all the rest of it, my good old Irish pastor said to me, he said, 'I'll just give you one piece of advice. People don't care how much you know. They want to know if you know them.' And that always stuck with me. I think that it's true in this case too. We don't go and give people the *Catechism* right away and say, 'Here, learn this.' They want to know if we know them and their lives and their circumstances. And this is the great mission and the approach that the Holy Father is saying when he says we need to encounter, we need to accompany, and we need to integrate people."

—Cardinal Blase Cupich, Archbishop of Chicago

In *Young Catholic America*, Christian Smith and his team of sociologists demonstrate that three primary factors in the teen years have a strong impact on young adult spirituality and healthy life choices: having close relationships with religiously committed family and friends (especially parents and mentors), internalizing Catholic beliefs, and having regular religious practices.[4] The Springtide Research Institute likewise corroborates the strong role mentors play in religiosity and positive life outcomes.[5] For instance, they found that among Catholic youth and young adults who report having zero adult mentors, 57 percent say their life has meaning and purpose. Among those who report having five or more mentors, this figure jumps to 91 percent. In my book *Young Adult American Catholics*, a variety of young adult Catholic subpopulations (e.g., undergrads, Hispanic) are explored using both scholarly research and voices from young adults themselves.[6] I demonstrate the variety of ways the church can better support young people as they discern where God is calling them. In an inter-religious study, theologian Donna Freitas documents that, despite the large number of college undergrads who do not identify with any religious tradition, nearly all of them identify as spiritual and are hoping to fulfill significant spiritual and human longings.[7] All in all, there are a good number of scholarly resources for people to consider as they craft ministries for Catholic youth and young adults.

There are a few things that these findings point to for meaningful pastoral practices. Beginning with the *Going, Going, Gone* finding that some leave because they disagree with church teaching, it is important that youth and young adults know—as was discussed earlier in the book—that part of being a loyal Catholic includes engaging with church teaching. You can even disagree with teachings; disagreement does not make you a less faithful Catholic according to respondents, as 89 percent of cultural Catholics and 85 percent of frequent attenders claim this. Again, while this seems to be a given for older Catholics, younger Catholics do not seem to have the same facility and seem to think that they must leave if they disagree with church teaching.[8] Along with this, the primacy of conscience in the Catholic moral life should be taught at the outset, but systematically so in Catholic high schools and confirmation programs—and again, not just taught, but exercises that involve reflecting on past, present, and future choices and how these reflect the dignity of or depart from the person's conscience would help make this a formative experience. Similarly, as high school and college students and young adults are discerning major life choices, from dating to college to career, skills and practices that guide Catholic discernment would also be very relevant tools for this group. Again, although 64 percent of cultural Catholics pray when faced with an important decision, this is much lower than the 90 percent of frequently attending Catholics who say this. The more that their experience of Catholicism meets their actual needs, the more firmly they will identify the tradition as something meaningful and life giving.

Looking back at another piece of data, 62 percent of cultural Catholics say that the sacraments are important to their relationship with God. Although this is a sizable majority, this is a far cry from the 92 percent of frequently attending Catholics who say this. Parents and ministers would be wise to talk to Catholics as young as possible not just about the connections between God and the sacraments, but what it means to see the world with a sacramental imagination, which makes the sacraments relevant to our everyday lives. This means, for example, knowing not simply that God is in the Eucharist, but also that the Eucharist shows how deeply God loves us and wants to be with us; this can be very formative. To draw eucharistic comparisons to God's love with more direct experiences in our own lives (e.g., blessed, broken, and shared) would help people wrap their heads around this. To know that in Communion we are united to God and one another is a powerful experience, and it also includes coming to realize that the Eucharist provides an ethics for everyday life that commits us to the poor and challenges us to orient ourselves toward others. And this is to focus only on the Eucharist. The seven sacraments all are visible signs of God's invisible grace. How does this offer us a sacramental imagination that might more readily see God's in-breaking? As we provide opportunities for people to sit in mystery, we evoke wonder and awe and can transform the imaginations of others.

Another insight for youth and young adult programming is to better include Catholic social teaching. Recalling the vignette featuring Cynthia, the young adult who was starting to feel estranged from her faith because it was silent on her political commitments (little did she know it was not, but church ministers simply failed to highlight these), this reminds us that many young adults are committed to a variety of political causes that are aligned with progressive politics, like migration, racial justice, systemic causes of poverty, and climate change. However, perhaps owing to media coverage, these stances are less well-known by many. Not to in any way discount the more conservative positions the church takes on same-sex marriage and abortion, because these positions are more widely known, Republican-leaning Catholics can more easily feel like they have a political home within Catholicism than their Democratically leaning counterparts. It is also wise to note here that becoming more politically vocal does not mean becoming more partisan. This is an important distinction that must be top of mind in these polarized times.[9]

Many young adults want to "do something." They want to get involved in supporting a *cause* even while they shy away from *institutions*. The more parishes or other faith-based groups can offer opportunities to put their faith into action, the more relevant parishes will feel to youth, young adults, and other Catholics who want their faith to matter to their everyday lives and world. This is another reminder to keep a parish's mission center stage as leaders think through programs and identity.

This connection between faith and everyday life must not be understated. In their study of religiosity among those in their twenties, sociologists Tim Clydesdale and Kathleen Garces-Foley found that whether a Catholic was "active," "nominal," or "estranged" was connected to a number of survey questions that connected faith and everyday life.[10] Active Catholics are more likely than nominal or estranged Catholics to believe they have an obligation to help others even if it means personal sacrifice, to say that their deep passion is social justice, and to say that their religious faith is "extremely" or "very" important in shaping how they live their daily life. As people are better able to make these connections between their faith and their world, their attachment to Catholicism increases.

"Look at programs from a young adult perspective. Having opportunities where the church is not in the church [building], like meeting at a restaurant or a pub and just having people act as people without the church agenda. I think that's usually a safe space for people to reengage with the church. Not like a Theology on Tap thing but for these cultural Catholics that just come in and out to really keep a relationship with them. And to not necessarily have the church passively waiting, but to take an active role, whether that is through invitations through the use of social media and using that effectively and well. Again, it would be great if we had sponsor parishioners that can reach out to these people and have relationships built, so that the church just isn't necessarily the priest or the parish staff person working. Yeah, I think if we could extend our reach, and show hospitality in its various forms, whether that is food or making it so convenient, whatever you can do to make life easier, even if that means, 'Hey you want to have like a Zoom call? Just chat for five minutes? I just want to get to know you, maybe get to know your week.' I think that's better than saying, 'Oh, just come to Mass.' "

—John Michael Reyes, Director of Adult Spirituality,
St. Ignatius College Preparatory

Also, rather than simply waiting for irregularly attending Catholics to show up, campus ministries, youth groups, and parishes should host efforts that could attract folks beyond the usual suspects, such as movie nights, running clubs, or workshops on saving for retirement or paying off student loans. Thinking about programming that would meet needs beyond the explicitly spiritual is a rarity. An example of a ministry that does go beyond the overtly spiritual is a men's ministry called I Thirst. They meet monthly at a local brewery, and the one rule is that the men do not talk about God or faith. The ministry is intended to help men, religious and nonreligious, foster intimacy and quality friendship with other men. Many of the men attend the same parish, so a "How did you all meet?" inquiry invariably comes up, at which point the new member is told that he is always welcome to join them any Sunday for Mass, an upcoming event, and so forth. But, regardless of his interest in joining them for these, belonging to the group is kept primary.

A key liability to Catholic formation is that it is culturally expected (or, more honestly, required) only for the reception of sacraments. This means that often even infrequent attenders will come so that their child may receive baptism, First Communion, and (sometimes) confirmation—which is great—but it also means that even regular attenders neglect to send their child for ongoing formation in the years between sacraments (and that parents themselves do not often participate in adult formation). The merits of whole-family catechesis are becoming the consensus in pastoral circles. But for parishes in which this is not an option (e.g., there is not adequate staff or properly trained volunteers to shift all programming into this model), working hard to make formation relational has huge payoffs for engagement. In his study of small Catholic communities, Bernard Lee found that among Catholics who begin a small group, the explicit topic of the group (e.g., Bible study) is why they initially join, but the relationships they have formed are why they stay.[11] Creating formation programs for youth and their parents, marriage prep for young adults, and more that connects people to one another in meaningful ways increases the likelihood that they will continue to stay with a group. Other studies have shown that being in religious education classes as a teen has no bearing on adult religiosity, while being in a teen youth group does have a positive impact.[12] Thinking about this for a high school confirmation program, a university student retreat, or marriage prep means integrating experiences to socialize, play, and otherwise encounter one another. All programming must be done well, especially required programs, as this might be the one chance we have to invite this youth or young adult to encounter God and the Catholic faith.

"It is a staggering reality when [RCIA and confirmation] should be a trigger moment. Where all of these Catholic moments, these sacramental moments, should be moments where we win people forever. And unfortunately, they are not. And in fact, in many cases, the complete opposite happens. We actually lose people through these trigger moments. Because if something like confirmation is not done well—See, the student comes usually in their late teens. They come and very often the culture has said to them, 'The church has nothing to offer.' If we do not do that moment well, we confirm that bias. And they walk away from confirmation saying the church has nothing to offer. And so the stakes are enormously high on things like that."

—Matthew Kelly, Founder, Dynamic Catholic

This also signals that youth and young adult programming often suffer from a "cold handoff." Too often a First Communion (or confirmation or marriage prep) program ends abruptly after "the big day." I know that my own daughter came to really enjoy the eight other companions who were formed with her in first and second grades for her First Communion experience. If the elementary youth group leader had participated in the last few months of sacramental prep, I am sure more would have made the leap into that youth group. The same can be said for the transition from elementary youth group into middle school youth group, into confirmation, into high school youth group, and so on, with meaningful mentor relationships the whole way. And while each of these transitions is critical, this is especially the case for the transition from high school into college and from college into "the real world."

As it is now, most institutions (e.g., Catholic high schools and universities, parishes, Newman Centers) practice a cold handoff. Students are bid farewell at one institution and they have, perhaps, only the coaxing of their parents to wander into their college campus ministry. They have a similar experience when they graduate and possibly look for a parish that resonates with their own Catholicity. Imagine instead that high school youth group leaders or, for Catholic high schools, campus ministers worked more closely with the graduating students and their new universities for a "warm handoff." Gabriel, for example, is at a Catholic high school and is going to a small liberal arts school for college. Patty, his campus minister, investigates his options (with the permission of Gabriel and his parents, of course). She discovers that there is no Newman Center at his small campus, but there is a Catholic student association on campus as well as a parish that has a sizable young adult group. She contacts the leaders of each of these and arranges with them and Gabriel's family to have lunch together the day after Gabriel arrives. The student leader has a printout of the major events they have that semester, and they exchange phone numbers. The parish young adult leader does the same and, when she discovers that Gabriel plays the guitar, asks if he wouldn't mind offering his talents in the praise team, which meets one Friday per month, starting this Friday. Gabriel, who was feeling anxious about being a stranger in a new place, happily accepts the invitation. Gabriel did not slip through the ministerial cracks, as can happen in a cold handoff. When he graduates four years from now, the parish minister does the same thing so that he is warmly welcomed into a thriving young adult community when he relocates for his first job.

Parishes

Thirty-seven percent of frequent attenders believe parishes are too big and impersonal (still too many, I say) and this rises to half of cultural Catholics. Compared to most Protestant churches, Catholic churches are very large. One of the most effective ways to create a sense of intimacy in a large parish is to have small groups, but with thinly spread priests and staff, this can also be a challenge. In the case of understaffing, be patient. It can be worse to rush into creating small groups with poorly trained small-group leaders than it is to postpone these. Start with what you have. If you have four people who can run small groups well (e.g., they facilitate the conversation rather than filling silence or pontificating with a mini-homily), start with four and pair them off for two groups. These small-group leaders will identify others within their groups who can act as facilitators for future groups. Creating small groups that personalize the parish experience and foster a sense of intimacy is key. Begin with just a handful of very meaningful small groups. Odds are that most people who have a meaningful small-group experience will want to share this with others.

But what about those who do not attend small groups? First, reduce friction. There are two ways to accomplish any goal you set out to do: adding fuel (putting in more energy) or reducing friction (removing obstacles). Typically, we think in the "add fuel" mindset. That is, we put more and more energy toward a goal until it gets accomplished. For example, we are a mattress company and we have thousands of dollars in ads everywhere about our mattresses, but we are not seeing much of an uptick in purchases. We start knocking on doors and we come to learn that people are reluctant to purchase a new mattress because they are unsure how to dispose of the old one. Our ads are set to expire and we renew one-fourth of them, with a large addition to the ad as well as a banner outside our storefront reading, "Free mattress disposal included!" The phones start ringing off the hook. Potential customers did not need us to add fuel, they needed us to reduce friction.

Parishes need to think along these lines. If you want people to come to something, have it in the forty-five-minute slot between Masses. Do not ask parents to come to middle school youth group on Wednesday and elementary school youth group on Thursday; it is hard for many to make two trips. Instead, hold both on the same evening. You could even hold a parent fellowship gathering at the same time—then childcare would be covered, too. Granted, not everything can flow so seamlessly, but it is a helpful reminder that adding fuel (through announcements and phone invitations) is not the only way to accomplish your ministerial goals.

Second, reshape programming so that it follows a small-group format. So if you have forty sacramental prep parents required to attend monthly meetings that consist of a one-hour "talk" followed by twenty minutes of small-group discussion, think about ways to make this small-group aspect dominant. Could the talk portion be reduced to twenty minutes? Could the talk be eliminated and experiential questions or Scripture discussions be the small-group focus? Could there be days where socializing and relationship building is the focus? Is there time for quiet reflection focused on a relevant question? My own confirmation program included about one hundred youth, but we all met in groups of eight in volunteers' homes for a shared curriculum that was nearly all discussion. We enjoyed it and we enjoyed each other. These two strategies, reducing friction and using the small-group format in required contexts, helps maximize the number of people who will experience small groups and, ideally, be more drawn into the parish community in a variety of ways.

"I think my immediate thought would be that parishes are big. The problem, though, is not really the size of the parish. The problem is that there aren't more apostolic laborers in the parish among the lay people. . . . If we have more laborers in the pews, the parishes—no matter how big they are—won't feel big because there will be more people in the pews equipped for this kind of personal engagement."

—Jason Simon, President, Evangelical Catholic

Recalling earlier data that the top reason cultural Catholics gave for not attending Mass more often was that it conflicted with work or family obligations may be key. It could be pivotal because, as the chapter on the nuances among cultural Catholics demonstrated, more than half of those who attend Mass a few times per year (53%) name this reason (only 39% of those who attend seldom or never say this). They come a few times per year, but either work or family get in the way. We admittedly do not know the full story here. Does the current Mass schedule actually conflict with set events (e.g., a busy sports schedule, weekend work shifts)? Or is it that people are simply so wiped out from chaotic schedules with work and kids' activities that they cannot imagine making it to church? Or is it that they just do not see how Mass might enhance their relationship to their job or the relationships within their family? There are probably folks who fit into each of these categories. The key for each parish is to figure out what is the case for the cultural Catholics in their parish territory and make a change.

As for the first question (that Mass conflicts with other activities, forcing families to choose between the two), many in ministry write this off. They figure that, yes, on occasion there is a true conflict, but most of the time people simply make time for what they want to make time for. But one of the interviewees I spoke with told an anecdote. Unbeknownst to the pastor, a good number of the parents of children in sacramental formation—many of whom never came to Mass—were also in the medical field and had to work weekends. When the pastor started talking to these parents, they said a 7:00 p.m. Mass would work for them. Six weeks after starting this new Mass, the 7:00 p.m. pews were full. There are situations in which there are real conflicts.

The second and third possibilities are different but could be addressed in similar ways. If people are exhausted from a full weekend or they do not see what "good" can come to their work or family in going to church, make the ways the parish supports work and family life front and center. Have workshops on recognizing and avoiding burnout or finding spiritual meaning in occupational vocation, and offer a "giftedness inventory" to see how people's talents and desires do and do not align with their employment. Have a family-centered Mass (even only monthly, if having these weekly does not make sense for your other parish needs). Make sure the deacon brings his own stories and spiritual insights gleaned from parenting into his homilies (priests should do the same in reflecting on how they admire their own parents' love of them). Create a space to socialize after Mass and make it inviting! I once knew a mom who, because she was a faith-based community organizer, rotated her Sunday Mass attendance across many parishes. She eventually had to stop doing this because her daughter absolutely loved going to St. Margaret's. Why? Barring rain, St. Margaret's turned on their "bounce house" after every 10:00 a.m. Mass. Rather than resisting going to Mass, her daughter looked forward to going to St. Margaret's. And her daughter quickly made good friends with the bounce-house regulars, as did the mother with the other parents who were keeping an eye on their children. Small choice, huge consequence.

On special occasions when the parish is getting more cultural Catholics than normal (e.g., Ash Wednesday, Christmas, Mother's Day, and Easter), it is much better to plan a liturgical and social experience that makes people want to come back than to try to cram a year of catechesis into a single homily. I once heard a Christmas Eve homily that hit creation, the Fall, incarnation, crucifixion, and resurrection all in ten minutes. But in just giving a quick nod to these, the priest said nothing at all. For Christmas, simply show people beauty, welcome, mystery, and joy; dive into the awe of the incarnation and invite them to a fun event at the parish coming up in two weekends . . . and some might come back. Odds are most will not, but perhaps your efforts will still leave them transformed in some small way and they will bring this with them into their world. Also be mindful that at events like weddings, baptisms, confirmations, and funerals, there will be a much greater percentage of cultural Catholics and non-Catholics in attendance. Bring good news to everyone present and awaken their spiritual longings and insights.

Parishes are also not tapping into people's inherent spiritual longings, nor making a compelling case that parish life is worth their time more than watching a sports game is. First, how is it that the Mass experiences they have had do not tap into their spiritual sensibilities? What are the topics or questions that priests and deacons are bringing to their homilies that fail to bring listeners' lives into an encounter with Jesus? I knew of a priest who wanted to make sure he was incorporating women's perspectives into his homily, so he had a group of women he would meet with on Monday mornings and they would go over the coming Sunday's readings together and reflect on these. Doing the same for a number of parish demographics on a rotating basis would help make sure the priest has a sense of the pulse of his listeners and can craft relevant homilies. Hearing in the homily an encounter with Scripture that connects with their lives could help people believe that they are, in fact, religious, and that attending Mass is worthwhile. Finally—and I have heard different things from a licensing perspective, so please research this—why not have an event after Mass where parishioners can socialize and watch the "big game" together (even if they might miss the first few minutes)? Parishes could even have a "Red Sox ministry," or whatever home team people get excited about, in which people meet for games at the parish or at a sports bar and can connect with parishioners over their shared loyalty to a team. This could also prove to be an effective intergenerational ministry as well.

As mentioned earlier, 38 percent of cultural Catholics are registered at a parish. This means parishes need to reach out to these people and see how they might serve them. This is perhaps the most untapped way of reaching cultural Catholics. Again, Pope

Francis has encouraged Catholics to think of the church as a "field hospital" that goes out, rather than that waits for people to come to parish grounds. Although knocking on every door in a parish territory would be the most thorough example of this, simply connecting with people registered at the parish but who are rarely in attendance is an easier and effective first step. We shouldn't lead with "Why don't you come to Mass?" But just begin by getting to know people and find out what sorts of activities they might be interested in. When, after enough visits to establish a trusting ministerial relationship, you do ask about why they stopped attending Mass, be ready to hear a variety of responses; some will report boredom, but others may have had a very negative experience. Listen with an open heart and thank them for their honesty.

"At RENEW we have a new process for baptism for when people come to have their children baptized because again, many of them are cultural Catholics, their grandmother or their mother wants the baby baptized, but make that the best experience, an evangelical experience. And instead of boring them to tears and telling them about all the rules and you know, how can that experience be 1) to help them have an encounter with Christ and 2) see that being engaged in the community is celebrating and receiving Eucharist can help them with their families and their children and those kinds of things."

—Sr. Theresa Rickard, OP, DMin,
President, RENEW International

We also need to do a better job of welcoming the occasional cultural Catholic who comes to us in key moments. Beyond just providing a more amazing parish experience on days when we are likely to have more cultural Catholics in the pews, we also have to be really hospitable when someone comes in asking about getting married, having their child baptized, wanting a confirmation certificate so they can be a godparent, and so forth. Some of these people may have not been to a church in years, and yet they have some beautiful event that they want to share with the church. Do not blow this by leading with, "So, are you registered at the parish?" Instead respond with, "Really? You're getting married!? That is wonderful, congratulations!" And celebrate with them. Show them that they and this event are a joy and a gift. Yes, there is paperwork and protocol, but that is something that follows your warm and heartfelt appreciation of them.

"I think the gateway moments are it, I really do. Because the cultural Catholics—here's what we see, at least from diocesan work and a little bit from ESTEEM. They're going to, more likely than not, probably want to get married in the church, maybe because grandma wants them to get married in the church or mom or whatever but more likely they'll get married in the church. They'll be at weddings, they'll be at funerals, they'll be at baptisms, so there's going to be all those gateway moments. They might then, because they are Catholic and their cousin's Catholic, be the godparents to their cousin's baby. So even though they might not be worshiping regularly, they're like, 'Okay that's an important thing. I gotta go to the parish and get some sort of piece of paper right to prove that I did—' Okay, these are all gateway moments, so if we acknowledge they come in those moments. What can we do to capture them? What can we do to say, 'Oh man, we're so glad you're here!' Let's make this as easy, joyful, celebratory as possible, as much as appropriate in each of those contacts. As opposed to saying, 'Oh well, you don't come here every single Sunday for Mass. I'm not going to sign your sponsor certificate.' Okay, well, great. Now any glimmer we had, any seed of hope we could have hoped to hang on to, we've now blown up. So, knowing that those gateway moments might be the only encounter we will have with them regularly and in any meaningful way, what can we do to bring them in deeper? So, is our marriage prep really, really strong or is our parish very hospitable, doing Disney-level hospitality? What does a sacramental preparation and other spheres—baptism, adult confirmation—look like? How can we invite them? Who's the person of encounter, is it just the parish secretary or—? Does the marriage prep team include young adult couples who can invite them deeper into other things? Or who's doing adult confirmation preparation and what else can they invite them to be a part of? Can small Christian communities become part of some of that preparation? All these million little ways, try stuff, but start in those gateway moments, because at least you have—They are coming to the door and they're coming in the door with a willing heart because they need something, and that's good. They need something of us as church, that's great, we want to be relevant. We don't get to define the parameters of relevance in each person's life. But when the moment comes, we get to choose what we do with it. So, in the moments that we're relevant, are we going to be backflips excited and joyful that they're here and like doing everything we can to make them feel like part of the community or are we gonna make it really hard and it's going to be slammed doors and hoops to jump through? Because then we will never be relevant again in their lives. But we see another chance if the welcome is strong."

—Nicole Perone, National Coordinator of ESTEEM,
Leadership Roundtable

Looking briefly to the whole sample, 44 percent of Catholics nationally believe parishes are too big and impersonal. This means nearly half of Catholics think parishes could stand to be more relational. This should indicate that, unless you have a parish that is stellar in this area, perhaps inviting your cultural Catholic cousin or coworker to Mass is not putting your parish's best foot forward. Instead, think about what your guest might get most excited about. Is it the Care for Creation ministry? Or perhaps it would be the Women's Guild's quarterly fundraiser lunch that has a high-tea vibe? A Bible study group? Or maybe a Christmas concert with some refreshments to follow? Whatever it is, just because you enjoy Mass at your parish does not mean that this is, necessarily, the ministry that is going to most ignite this person's spiritual side. Think about the particularities of your guest and be prudential in your invitation. Remember, you are just whetting an appetite and getting them excited for a second encounter.

Before we close out this parish section, it would be helpful to briefly revisit the assets of parishes: access, generalization and specialization, territory, and a space for encounter. Thinking through access, when people think about "the Catholic Church" they might envision some ideas or events that happen on a larger scale, but Catholics' real feelings about Catholicism tend to come from these parish (or Catholic school) experiences. If parishes could embody and project a positive image (e.g., compassionate care for the community) of themselves and their relationship with those in their territory, this would go far in helping parishes to become more attractive institutions. With regards to generalization and specialization, knowing what the parish territory and its cultural Catholics need and how these needs align with the gifts, mission, and talents of the parish is key. Conduct a synodal-style needs assessment of the active parishioners and have one-on-ones with those registered but not attending, and see how your parish might better serve those under its care. Parish as territory invites us to dream big and consider what sort of courageous act we might do that could proclaim the good news of Christ to the world. Encounter reminds us that parishes are places of formation in which we encounter God and one another and are formed and equipped to bring the good news to the world. We need to expand our imaginations and get excited.

Dioceses and Other Regional Efforts

This short section will explore pastoral takeaways for dioceses and other Catholic organizations that operate on a regional scale, like Catholic Charities, Young Catholic Professionals, a Catholic university and others. While I will use the word "dioceses" regularly, feel free to insert other institutional contexts as appropriate. There are two main considerations I want to offer here. The first is thinking about dioceses as training grounds for those in key parish roles—both lay staff and volunteer—to better equip those who are in ministerial roles. The second consideration is that these non-parish institutions may be the catalyst for a "seldom-or-never"-attending cultural Catholic (as opposed to the "few-times-per-year" attenders) to think more deeply about Catholicism.

Dioceses and other more regional institutions have the chance to better prepare Catholic ministers for encounters with cultural Catholics as well as to think through how they might be creative with their ministries so that they attract participants beyond the usual suspects. Thinking about the encounters with cultural Catholics, the parish receptionist, the wedding coordinator, those who prepare parents for the baptism of their child, the funeral coordinator, and others are going to be key mediators in cultural Catholics' experience of "the church." If a wedding coordinator is having a bad day and gets a tad snarky with a "stupid question" from the groom, that groom will probably not think "she was insensitive," but might process this as "the church was insensitive." In ministry, we need to always be aware of the impact our words and gestures have on others (and apologize sincerely when we fall short).

We also need to get creative about our ministries so that they might include irregular attenders. I heard great success from a parish that offered free babysitting (provided by confirmation teens needing service hours) to parents so they could go out on dates. It began as a way to support emotional connection between busy parents, but then it started to attract friends of parishioners as well. The kids would have a great time and would make friends with other kids at the parish. A next step could have been to offer a "free date" as well. Pasta, wine, salad, tiramisu, and fun conversation questions as a twosome could have helped those financially struggling (some parents' dates consisted of going home for wine and a movie). Suggesting that couples bring another couple for a double date with four at a table could also be very fun and touch even more lives.

But there is a lot going on in people's lives beyond date nights. Mental health, financial challenges, job dissatisfaction, addiction, tutoring and college readiness, unemployment, and more are also on the table. No one parish has the skills and resources to handle all these needs, but dioceses can pool or coordinate resources and discern how to meet the variety of needs of those in their care. Any human need, even those not explicitly spiritual, are the concerns of the church, and we need to show others we care about the whole of their personhood, not just a narrow piece of it. This is one of the many ways that the church can show that it is, in fact, relevant to people's lives.

"Jesus's fundamental model of ministry was to, essentially, never preach to anyone before he fed them, healed them, comforted them. He always dealt with a human need before he did the preaching. We have lost that as a church. We've lost our ability to connect and integrate the gospel with the real challenge of people's lives. And by doing that, we're losing those trigger experiences. Because if you are drowning in credit card debt and someone from the church comes and helps you overcome your credit card debt—they don't even talk about God, they don't talk about church, they don't ask you to come to church or tell you to go to church—they just say, 'Let us help you with your credit card debt. Let us help you think about it, get a plan.' That person is connected to that person and their church forever. It is an absolute trigger moment. It is a moment of inseparable connection. And if that person overcomes their credit card debt, it becomes an experience of gratitude that literally never ends. And so when we don't meet people where they're at, we're not able to create those trigger moments. Because the best way to win someone to the gospel is to show them how the gospel relates to the very worst part of their life. Because if it works there, it works everywhere."

—Matthew Kelly, Founder, Dynamic Catholic

The second consideration is that regional-level ministries are more likely to be visible in the media and so might be the one point of Catholic contact for those who attend seldom or never; the "few-times-a-year" folks are likely to be impressed by changes they encounter at the parish level when they do attend Mass. If parishes could make a bold or courageous move that would make a real difference in the world, how much more is that the case with a diocese? I think about my son's appreciation of the ways a famous YouTuber, MrBeast, engages in a number of philanthropic projects and how this inspires my son to contribute money to his efforts and get involved in causes. Why is Catholicism not causing the same level of "wow" as a YouTuber?

Imagine if a diocese were to say that no child would go hungry in their diocese. Parish or deanery food pantries would be well stocked with healthy food for any parent who could not put enough on the table. Parishioners would help run these through both donations and volunteering. No matter your political commitments, no one wants children to be hungry. This is an issue that everyone can get on board with. Anyone who heard of this would see this as good news. It could be the sort of thing that might get a never-attending Catholic involved one Saturday per month.

There also needs to be programming that can meet the spiritual needs of those who are not coming to church. At the risk of sounding redundant, having ministries that meet universal human needs like mental wellness are an important aspect of this. But it is also important to have spiritual resources available. Even after COVID, many parishes are continuing to stream their Masses online, which enables the homebound to have some sense of participation in the Mass even when their health requires them to remain at home. While an online Mass might not be the experience that helps some cultural Catholics feel connected to God, apps that help people practice gratitude, offer reminders to center themselves, start the day with *lectio divina*, end the day with an examen, and develop other prayer practices could be useful for those who still identify as Catholic but do not attend Mass. It is much easier for dioceses to build these sorts of resources than it is for a parish. And, rather than going to the national level with these, by staying relatively local, they can be made more relevant and can offer invitations to events.

I want to end this book with two final thoughts. First, I want to bring a Matthew Kelly interview quote directly into the text: "Friendship is the ultimate trigger. It is and always has been the best way to spread the faith." This is, perhaps, the most important thing to keep in mind as you consider not just the big parish programs, but the cultural Catholics in your life. Continue in loving friendship with them. And be sure that a no-strings-attached friendship is the central effort in building connections or staying connected with cultural Catholics. More than bringing cultural Catholics *into* the parish, parish programming should be helping Catholics in the pews to become more excited about their faith and more patient and caring *toward* the many people in their lives. Evangelization moves, pushes, and ripples outward. Authentic friendship is always good news and is bound to form all involved.

Second, what if after all these changes the cultural Catholics in our area and in our lives are still attending Mass at the same rates? Did we fail? That depends on your goal at the end of reading this book. I would say that if increasing Mass attendance is your goal, then yes, unfortunately, you failed. But if enlivening the faith and virtue of others was the goal, and you did this, then you succeeded. But what if, after a year or two, your coworker, your neighbor, your adult child . . . they are all still the same? Did you fail? I would hope that our goal is both bigger and simpler than transforming others. I think a central goal of the Christian life is to be faithful—to be faithful to God, to be faithful to the many relationships in our lives, to be faithful to the person we are growing into. And when fidelity is the goal—not an external outcome with many factors beyond our control—this goal will always enliven our own faith and virtue and will likely grow the hope of others. So, in closing this book, I ask that you make fidelity—to God, relationships, and self—your goal, that you work earnestly toward this, that you run the good race, that you let your faithfulness touch the lives of others and let this be the measure of your success.

Concluding Questions:

- What were the goals you started this book with? What are the goals you want to walk away with?

- What ideas discussed here could help you in your ministry with cultural Catholics? Did this book spark any other promising ideas within you?

- What are the elements of Catholicism that make your heart sing, enliven your spirit, or inspire you? How can these be brought to your various relationships? To your parish?

- Did you have a return to Catholicism? What were some of the people or events that prompted your return?

- Concretely, what can you commit to doing within the next seven days to bring the good news to others (even just one other)? Within the coming month? Within the year? Be courageous and don't fail to ask for help!

Notes

Acknowledgments

1. Maureen K. Day, James Cavendish, Paul M. Merl, Michele Dillon, Mary L. Gautier, with William V. D'Antonio, *Catholicism at a Crossroads* (New York: New York University Press, 2024); William V. D'Antonio, Michele Dillon, and Mary L. Gautier, *American Catholics in Transition* (Lanham, MD: Rowman & Littlefield, 2013); William V. D'Antonio, James D. Davidson, Dean R. Hoge, and Mary L. Gautier, *American Catholics Today* (Lanham, MD: Rowman & Littlefield, 2007); William V. D'Antonio, James D. Davidson, Dean R. Hoge, and Katherine Meyer, *American Catholics* (Walnut Creek, CA: AltaMira Press, 2001); William V. D'Antonio, James D. Davidson, Dean R. Hoge, and Ruth A. Wallace, *Laity, American and Catholic* (Kansas City, MO: Sheed & Ward, 1996); William V. D'Antonio, James D. Davidson, Dean R. Hoge, and Ruth A. Wallace, *American Catholic Laity in a Changing Church* (Kansas City, MO: Sheed and Ward, 1989).

Introduction

1. For a more in-depth discussion of the problems with these modifiers, including "cultural," see Tom Beaudoin, "Cultural Catholicism," in *The Cambridge Companion to American Catholicism*, ed. Margaret McGuinness and Thomas Rzeznik (New York: Cambridge University Press, 2021), 325–42.

2. My definition is similar to but still departs from that of practical theologian Tom Beaudoin, who defines cultural Catholics as those who were "baptized Catholic and do not make official Catholic teaching or practice a central part of their lives." An important distinction between my definition and Beaudoin's is that for him "cultural Catholics" may or may not themselves identify as Catholic, whereas all cultural Catholics in these pages do. Beaudoin, "Cultural Catholicism," in *Cambridge Companion to American Catholicism*, 327. Another use of "cultural Catholic" popular among academics at the time of this writing is to describe people who do *not* volunteer "Catholic" when asked about their religious affiliation, but who *do* agree with the statement, "Do you currently

consider yourself Catholic or partially Catholic in any way, or not?" This sense
of "cultural Catholic" has less of a religious identity quality to it (or else the
respondents would have volunteered "Catholic" when asked about their religion), and more of an ascribed identity quality, that is, an intrinsic aspect of
oneself. According to the Pew Research Center, using this understanding of
the term, roughly 9 percent of Americans meet this definition of "cultural
Catholic." For more on this, see "U.S. Catholics Open to Non-Traditional Families," Pew Research Center, September 2, 2015, https://www.pewresearch.org
/religion/2015/09/02/u-s-catholics-open-to-non-traditional-families/, accessed
March 27, 2023. See especially "Chapter 1: Exploring Catholic Identity" of the report here: https://www.pewresearch.org/religion/2015/09/02/chapter-1-exploring
-catholic-identity/, accessed March 27, 2023. See also David Masci, "Who Are
'Cultural Catholics'?," Pew Research Center, September 3, 2015, https://www
.pewresearch.org/fact-tank/2015/09/03/who-are-cultural-catholics/, accessed
March 27, 2023; and Tricia Colleen Bruce, "Cultural Catholics in the United
States," in *The Changing Faces of Catholicism*, ed. Solange Lefebvre and Alfonso
Pérez-Agote (Boston: Brill, 2018), 83–106.

3. Mark M. Gray, "Stable Transformation: Catholic Parishioners in the United
States," in *American Parishes: Remaking Local Catholicism*, ed. Gary J. Adler
Jr., Tricia Colleen Bruce, and Brian M. Starks (New York: Fordham University
Press, 2019), 99.

4. Charles E. Zech, Mary L. Gautier, Mark M. Gray, Jonathon L. Wiggins, and
Thomas P. Gaunt, SJ, *Catholic Parishes of the 21st Century* (New York: Oxford,
2017), 40.

5. *Catechism of the Catholic Church*, 2nd ed. (United States Catholic Conference
—Libreria Editrice Vaticana, 1997), no. 1324.

6. Tom Beaudoin, "Secular Catholicism and Practical Theology," *International
Journal of Practical Theology* 15, no. 1 (2011): 22–37.

7. To better understand the racial composition of Catholics, especially this
"other" category, data from the Pew Research Center is helpful. In 2014, they
found the racial breakdown of American Catholics to be 59 percent white, 34
percent Hispanic, 3 percent Black, 3 percent Asian, and 2 percent "other." It is
likely that the majority of those classified as "other" in our dataset would have
identified as Asian had the survey offered this category. Pew data comes from
Michael Lipka, "A Closer Look at Catholic America," Pew Research Center,
September 14, 2015, https://www.pewresearch.org/fact-tank/2015/09/14/a-closer
-look-at-catholic-america, accessed March 28, 2023.

Chapter 1

1. For more on the survey questions that are examined in this book, consult the many books from the D'Antonio series that began in the 1980s. Some of the more recent books include Maureen K. Day, James C. Cavendish, Paul M. Perl, Michele Dillon, and Mary L. Gautier with William V. D'Antonio, *Catholicism's Crossroads: The Present and Future of America's Largest Church* (New York: New York University Press, forthcoming); William V. D'Antonio, Michele Dillon, and Mary L. Gautier, *American Catholics in Transition* (Lanham, MD: Rowman and Littlefield, 2013); William V. D'Antonio, James D. Davidson, Dean R. Hoge, and Mary L. Gautier, *American Catholics Today: New Realities of Their Faith and Their Church* (Lanham, MD: Rowman and Littlefield, 2007); and William V. D'Antonio, James D. Davidson, Dean R. Hoge, and Katherine Meyer, *American Catholics: Gender, Generation, and Commitment* (Lanham, MD: Rowman and Littlefield, 2001).

2. For more on the ways parents pass their faith to their children, see Christian Smith, Bridget Ritz, and Michael Rotolo, *Religious Parenting: Transmitting Faith and Values in Contemporary America* (Princeton, NJ: Princeton University Press, 2020); and Christian Smith and Amy Adamczyk, *Handing Down the Faith: How Parents Pass Their Religion on to the Next Generation* (New York: Oxford University Press, 2021).

3. Jerome P. Baggett, *Sense of the Faithful: How American Catholics Live Their Faith* (New York: Oxford University Press, 2009), 82–88.

4. Michele Dillon, *Catholic Identity: Balancing Reason, Faith, and Power* (Boston: Cambridge University Press, 1999), 207.

Chapter 2

1. See literature review and authors' analysis in the "Trends" chapter in Maureen K. Day, James C. Cavendish, Paul M. Perl, Michele Dillon, and Mary L. Gautier with William V. D'Antonio, *Catholicism's Crossroads: The Present and Future of America's Largest Church* (New York: New York University Press, forthcoming). See also Mark Chaves, *American Religion: Contemporary Trends* (Princeton, NJ: Princeton University Press, 2011).

2. Robert D. Putnam and David E. Campbell, *American Grace: How Religion Divides and Unites Us* (New York: Simon & Schuster, 2010).

3. James D. Davidson, Andrea S. Williams, Richard A. Lamana, Jan Stenftenagel, Kathleen Weigert, William Whalen, and Patricia Wittberg, *The Search for Common Ground: What Unites and Divides Catholic Americans* (Huntington, IN: Our Sunday Visitor Press, 1997). Mary Ellen Konieczny, *The Spirit's Tether: Family, Work, and Religion among American Catholics* (New York: Oxford University Press, 2013). Mary Ellen Konieczny, Charles C. Camosy, Tricia C. Bruce, eds.,

Polarization in the US Catholic Church: Naming the Wounds, Beginning to Heal (Collegeville, MN: Liturgical Press, 2016).

4. Andrew Greeley, *The Catholic Imagination* (Berkeley: University of California Press, 2001).

5. Pope Francis, *Evangelii Gaudium* (The Joy of the Gospel), 2013, no. 14, https://www.vatican.va/content/francesco/en/apost_exhortations/documents/papa-francesco_esortazione-ap_20131124_evangelii-gaudium.html, accessed December 21, 2023. Italics in original in this and the quote in the following sentence.

6. Shankar Vedantam, "Where Gratitude Gets You," interview with David DeSteno, *Hidden Brain*, podcast audio, no date, https://hiddenbrain.org/podcast/where-gratitude-gets-you.

7. Putnam and Campbell, *American Grace*.

8. I do not want to overlook the key philosophical tradition within Franciscan thought as formulated by St. Bonaventure and Duns Scotus, which traces its roots to St. Augustine and Plato. However, given the scope of this work and that Pope Leo XIII's 1879 *Aeterni Patris* established Thomism as the dominant philosophical tradition of Catholicism, I will leave the reader to discover the distinctions and complements of the Franciscan approach to virtue ethics elsewhere. I assure you that it is a worthwhile endeavor and suggest the following as a first source: Thomas Nairn, *The Franciscan Moral Vision: Responding to God's Love* (St. Bonaventure, NY: Franciscan Institute, 2013).

9. Depending upon the English translation one has, the original Greek is most commonly translated as "blessed" or "happy."

10. Christian Smith and Hilary Davidson, *The Paradox of Generosity: Giving We Receive, Grasping We Lose* (New York: Oxford University Press, 2014).

Chapter 3

1. For this and many other fascinating facts about contemporary parish life, see Charles E. Zech, Mary L. Gautier, Mark M. Gray, Jonathon L. Wiggins, and Thomas P. Gaunt, SJ, *Catholic Parishes of the 21ˢᵗ Century* (New York: Oxford, 2017), 26.

2. Claire Gecewicz and Dennis Quinn, "U.S. Churchgoers Are Satisfied with the Sermons They Hear, Though Content Varies by Religious Tradition," Pew Research Center, January 28, 2020, https://www.pewresearch.org/short-reads/2020/01/28/u-s-churchgoers-are-satisfied-with-the-sermons-they-hear-though-content-varies-by-religious-tradition.

3. *Catechism of the Catholic Church*, nos. 1776–94. This section of the *Catechism* also cites the famous line from *Gaudium et Spes*, "Conscience is the most secret core and sanctuary of a man. There he is alone with God, Whose voice echoes in his depths" (no. 16).

4. National Conference of Catholic Bishops, "Human Life in Our Day," Pastoral Letter, 1968, https://www.ewtn.com/catholicism/library/human-life-in-our-day-3895.

5. Dean R. Hoge, William D. Dinges, Mary Johnson, and Juan L. Gonzales Jr., *Young Adult Catholics: Religion in the Culture of Choice* (Notre Dame, IN: University of Notre Dame Press, 2001), 198–99.

6. Robert J. McCarty and John M. Vitek, *Going, Going, Gone: The Dynamics of Disaffiliation in Young Catholics* (Winona, MN: Saint Mary's Press, 2018), 21–24.

7. When it comes to accommodations Catholics are willing to accept given the priest shortage, they are least supportive of decreasing priestly care surrounding issues of sickness and death; see William V. D'Antonio, James D. Davidson, Dean R. Hoge, and Katherine Meyer, *American Catholics: Gender, Generation, and Commitment* (Lanham, MD: Rowman & Littlefield, 2001), 106.

8. Zech et al., *Catholic Parishes of the 21ˢᵗ Century*, 37.

9. I have had people approach me with a variety of comments or questions that they insist are Catholic: believing that being pro-life politically is *only* about restricting access to abortion, not also about passing legislation that supports women and families; that God wills people to sin in the world as a way of testing others and helping us to grow stronger; or that a clandestinely stolen piece of the Shroud of Turin was tested and "proves" Jesus's existence as well as the virgin birth because the blood sample only had one set of chromosomes. I try my best to respond to people in a way that reveals God's love and goodness while still trying to shepherd people closer into Catholic teaching, all while staying cool! Hats off to full-time ministers who field these sorts of things on the daily!

10. John C. Seitz, *No Closure: Catholic Practice and Boston's Parish Shutdowns* (Cambridge, MA: Harvard University Press, 2011).

11. Attitudes toward religion broadly can be found in Pew Research Center, "Chapter 2: Attitudes toward Organized Religion," *The Religious Typology*, August 28, 2018, https://www.pewresearch.org/religion/2018/08/29/attitudes-toward-organized-religion-2. The Catholic-specific data comes from Patricia Tevington, "Americans Feel More Positive Than Negative about Jews, Mainline Protestants, Catholics," March 15, 2023, https://www.pewresearch.org/religion/2023/03/15/americans-feel-more-positive-than-negative-about-jews-mainline-protestants-catholics.

12. Christian Smith and Michael O. Emerson with Patricia Snell, *Passing the Plate: Why American Christians Don't Give Away More Money* (New York: Oxford University Press, 2008), 53.

13. Pope Francis, "For a Culture of Encounter," Morning Meditation in the Chapel of the *Domus Sanctae Marthae*, September 13, 2016, https://www.vatican.va/content/francesco/en/cotidie/2016/documents/papa-francesco-cotidie_20160913_for-a-culture-of-encounter.html/, accessed April 14, 2022.

14. Susan Bigelow Reynolds, *People Get Ready: Ritual, Solidarity, and Lived Ecclesiology in Catholic Roxbury* (New York: Fordham University Press, 2023).

15. *Catechism of the Catholic Church*, nos. 1396–97.

16. Robert D. Putnam and David E. Campbell, *American Grace: How Religion Divides and Unites Us* (New York: Simon & Schuster, 2010), 477.

17. Robert Wuthnow, *Sharing the Journey: Support Groups and America's New Quest for Community* (New York: The Free Press, 1996).

18. Bernard J. Lee, *The Catholic Experience of Small Christian Communities* (Mahwah, NJ: Paulist Press, 2000), 130–33.

19. Patricia Ewick and Marc W. Steinberg, *Beyond Betrayal: The Priest Sex Abuse Crisis, the Voice of the Faithful, and the Process of Collective Identity* (Chicago: University of Chicago Press, 1996); Christian Smith, *Resisting Reagan: The U.S. Central America Peace Movement* (Chicago: University of Chicago Press, 1996), 181; Jerome Baggett, *Habitat for Humanity: Building Private Homes, Building Public Religion* (Philadelphia: Temple University Press, 2000), 135; Bin Xu, *The Politics of Compassion: The Sichuan Earthquake and Civic Engagement in China* (Stanford, CA: Stanford University Press, 2017); and Maureen K. Day, *Catholic Activism Today: Individual Transformation and the Struggle for Social Justice* (New York: New York University Press, 2020), 159.

Chapter 4

1. Maureen K. Day, "Polarization? Identifying What Unites and Divides American Catholics," *Politics and Religion* 17, no. 2 (2023): 251–75.

2. Robert Putnam, *Bowling Alone: The Collapse and Revival of American Community* (New York: Simon & Schuster, 2000); Robert D. Putnam and David E. Campbell, *American Grace: How Religion Divides and Unites Us* (New York: Simon & Schuster, 2010); and Pew Research Center, "Religion's Relationship to Happiness, Civic Engagement and Health Around the World," January 31, 2019, https://www.pewforum.org/2019/01/31/religions-relationship-to-happiness -civic-engagement-and-health-around-the-world.

Chapter 5

1. This analysis would be further enhanced by reading the "Church" chapter in Maureen K. Day, James C. Cavendish, Paul M. Perl, Michele Dillon, and Mary L. Gautier with William V. D'Antonio, *Catholicism's Crossroads: The Present and Future of America's Largest Church* (New York: New York University Press, forthcoming).

2. Tom Beaudoin, "Cultural Catholicism," in *The Cambridge Companion to American Catholicism*, ed. Margaret McGuinness and Thomas Rzeznik (New York: Cambridge University Press, 2021), 333.

3. Robert J. McCarty and John M. Vitek, *Going, Going, Gone: The Dynamics of Disaffiliation in Young Catholics* (Winona, MN: Saint Mary's Press, 2018).

4. Christian Smith, Kyle Longest, Jonathan Hill, and Kari Christoffersen, *Young Catholic America: Emerging Adults In, Out of, and Gone from the Church* (New York: Oxford University Press, 2014).

5. Springtide Research Institute, *The State of Religion and Young People: Relational Authority*, Catholic Edition (Winona, MN: Springtide Research Institute, 2020).

6. Maureen K. Day, ed., *Young Adult American Catholics: Explaining Vocation in Their Own Words* (Mahwah, NJ: Paulist Press, 2018).

7. Donna Freitas, *Sex and the Soul: Juggling Sexuality, Spirituality, Romance, and Religion on America's College Campuses* (New York: Oxford University Press, 2008).

8. See also Dean R. Hoge, William D. Dinges, Mary Johnson, and Juan L. Gonzales Jr., *Young Adult Catholics: Religion in the Culture of Choice* (Notre Dame, IN: University of Notre Dame Press, 2001), 198–99.

9. A more in-depth discussion of Catholicism and American politics can be found in the "Citizenship" chapter in Day et al., *Catholicism's Crossroads*, forthcoming.

10. Tim Clydesdale and Kathleen Garces-Foley, *The Twentysomething Soul: Understanding the Religious and Secular Lives of American Young Adults* (New York: Oxford University Press, 2019).

11. Bernard J. Lee with William V. D'Antonio, Virgilio P. Elizondo, Patricia O'Connell Killen, and Jeanette Rodriguez, *The Catholic Experience of Small Christian Communities* (New York: Paulist Press, 2000), 44, 71.

12. Andrew M. Greeley, William C. McCready, and Kathleen McCourt, *Catholic Schools in a Declining Church* (Kansas City, MO: Sheed & Ward, 1976). Paul Perl and Mark M. Gray, "Catholic Schooling and Disaffiliation from Catholicism," *Journal for the Scientific Study of Religion* 46 (2007): 269–80.

Bibliography

Baggett, Jerome. *Habitat for Humanity: Building Private Homes, Building Public Religion*. Philadelphia: Temple University Press, 2000.

Baggett, Jerome P. *Sense of the Faithful: How American Catholics Live Their Faith*. New York: Oxford University Press, 2009.

Beaudoin, Tom. "Secular Catholicism and Practical Theology." *International Journal of Practical Theology* 15, no. 1 (2011): 22–37.

Beaudoin, Tom. "Cultural Catholicism." In *The Cambridge Companion to American Catholicism*, edited by Margaret McGuinness and Thomas Rzeznik, 325–342. New York: Cambridge University Press, 2021.

Bruce, Tricia Colleen. "Cultural Catholics in the United States." In *The Changing Faces of Catholicism*, edited by Solange Lefebvre and Alfonso Pérez-Agote, 83–106. Boston: Brill, 2018.

Catechism of the Catholic Church. 2nd ed. United States Catholic Conference—Libreria Editrice Vaticana, 1997.

Chaves, Mark. *American Religion: Contemporary Trends*. Princeton, NJ: Princeton University Press, 2011.

Clydesdale, Tim, and Kathleen Garces-Foley. *The Twentysomething Soul: Understanding the Religious and Secular Lives of American Young Adults*. New York: Oxford University Press, 2019.

D'Antonio, William V., James D. Davidson, Dean R. Hoge, and Mary L. Gautier. *American Catholics Today: New Realities of Their Faith and Their Church*. Lanham, MD: Rowman and Littlefield, 2007.

D'Antonio, William V., Michele Dillon, and Mary L. Gautier. *American Catholics in Transition*. Lanham, MD: Rowman and Littlefield, 2013.

D'Antonio, William V., James D. Davidson, Dean R. Hoge, and Katherine Meyer. *American Catholics: Gender, Generation, and Commitment*. Lanham, MD: Rowman and Littlefield, 2001.

Davidson, James D., Andrea S. Williams, Richard A Lamana, Jan Stenftenagel, Kathleen Weigert, William Whalen, and Patricia Wittberg. *The Search for Common Ground: What Unites and Divides Catholic Americans.* Huntington, IN: Our Sunday Visitor Press, 1997.

Day, Maureen K., ed. *Young Adult American Catholics: Explaining Vocation in Their Own Words.* Mahwah, NJ: Paulist Press, 2018.

Day, Maureen K. *Catholic Activism Today: Individual Transformation and the Struggle for Social Justice.* New York: New York University Press, 2020.

Day, Maureen K. "Polarization? Identifying What Unites and Divides American Catholics." *Politics and Religion* 17, no. 2 (2023): 251–75.

Day, Maureen K., James C. Cavendish, Paul M. Perl, Michele Dillon, and Mary L. Gautier with William V. D'Antonio. *Catholicism's Crossroads: The Present and Future of America's Largest Church.* New York: New York University Press, forthcoming.

Dillon, Michele. *Catholic Identity: Balancing Reason, Faith, and Power.* Boston: Cambridge University Press, 1999.

Ewick, Patricia, and Marc W. Steinberg. *Beyond Betrayal: The Priest Sex Abuse Crisis, the Voice of the Faithful, and the Process of Collective Identity.* Chicago: University of Chicago Press, 1996.

Freitas, Donna. *Sex and the Soul: Juggling Sexuality, Spirituality, Romance, and Religion on America's College Campuses.* New York: Oxford University Press, 2008.

Gecewicz, Claire, and Dennis Quinn. "U.S. Churchgoers Are Satisfied with the Sermons They Hear, Though Content Varies by Religious Tradition." Pew Research Center, January 28, 2020. https://www.pewresearch.org/short-reads/2020/01/28/u-s-churchgoers-are-satisfied-with-the-sermons-they-hear-though-content-varies-by-religious-tradition/.

Gray, Mark M. "Stable Transformation: Catholic Parishioners in the United States." In *American Parishes: Remaking Local Catholicism,* edited by Gary J. Adler Jr., Tricia Colleen Bruce, and Brian M. Starks, 95–107. New York: Fordham University Press, 2019.

Greeley, Andrew. *The Catholic Imagination.* Berkeley: University of California Press, 2001.

Greeley, Andrew M., William C. McCready, and Kathleen McCourt. *Catholic Schools in a Declining Church.* Kansas City, MO: Sheed & Ward, 1976.

Hoge, Dean R., William D. Dinges, Mary Johnson, and Juan L. Gonzales Jr. *Young Adult Catholics: Religion in the Culture of Choice.* Notre Dame, IN: University of Notre Dame Press, 2001.

Konieczny, Mary Ellen. *The Spirit's Tether: Family, Work, and Religion among American Catholics.* New York: Oxford University Press, 2013.

Konieczny, Mary Ellen, Charles C. Camosy, and Tricia C. Bruce, eds. *Polarization in the US Catholic Church: Naming the Wounds, Beginning to Heal.* Collegeville, MN: Liturgical Press, 2016.

Lee, Bernard J. *The Catholic Experience of Small Christian Communities.* Mahwah, NJ: Paulist Press, 2000.

Lipka, Michael. "A Closer Look at Catholic America." Pew Research Center, September 14, 2015. https://www.pewresearch.org/fact-tank /2015/09/14/a-closer-look-at-catholic-america/.

Masci, David. "Who Are 'Cultural Catholics'?" Pew Research Center, September 3, 2015. https://www.pewresearch.org/fact-tank/2015/09/03 /who-are-cultural-catholics/.

McCarty, Robert J., and John M. Vitek. *Going, Going, Gone: The Dynamics of Disaffiliation in Young Catholics.* Winona, MN: Saint Mary's Press, 2018.

Nairn, Thomas. *The Franciscan Moral Vision: Responding to God's Love.* St. Bonaventure, NY: Franciscan Institute, 2013.

National Conference of Catholic Bishops. "Human Life in Our Day." Pastoral Letter. November 15, 1968. https://www.ewtn.com/catholicism /library/human-life-in-our-day-3895/.

Perl, Paul and Mark M. Gray. "Catholic Schooling and Disaffiliation from Catholicism." *Journal for the Scientific Study of Religion* 46 (2007): 269–280.

Pew Research Center. "U.S. Catholics Open to Non-Traditional Families." September 2, 2015. https://www.pewresearch.org/religion /2015/09/02/u-s-catholics-open-to-non-traditional-families/.

Pew Research Center. "Chapter 2: Attitudes toward Organized Religion." *The Religious Typology,* August 28, 2018. https://www.pewresearch .org/religion/2018/08/29/attitudes-toward-organized-religion-2/.

Pew Research Center. "Religion's Relationship to Happiness, Civic Engagement and Health Around the World." January 31, 2019. https:// www.pewforum.org/2019/01/31/religions-relationship-to-happiness -civic-engagement-and-health-around-the-world/.

Pope Francis. *Amoris Laetitia* (The Joy of Love). Vatican, March 19, 2016. https://www.vatican.va/content/francesco/en/apost_exhortations /documents/papa-francesco_esortazione-ap_20160319_amoris -laetitia.html.

Pope Francis. *Evangelii Gaudium* (The Joy of the Gospel). Vatican, November 24, 2013. https://www.vatican.va/content/francesco/en/apost _exhortations/documents/papa-francesco_esortazione-ap_20131124 _evangelii-gaudium.html.

Pope Francis. "For a Culture of Encounter." Morning Meditation in the Chapel of the *Domus Sanctae Marthae*. September 13, 2016. https:// www.vatican.va/content/francesco/en/cotidie/2016/documents /papa-francesco-cotidie_20160913_for-a-culture-of-encounter.html/.

Putnam, Robert. *Bowling Alone: The Collapse and Revival of American Community*. New York: Simon & Schuster, 2000.

Putnam, Robert D., and David E. Campbell. *American Grace: How Religion Divides and Unites Us*. New York: Simon & Schuster, 2010.

Reynolds, Susan Bigelow. *People Get Ready: Ritual, Solidarity, and Lived Ecclesiology in Catholic Roxbury*. New York: Fordham University Press, 2023.

Seitz, John C. *No Closure: Catholic Practice and Boston's Parish Shutdowns*. Cambridge, MA: Harvard University Press, 2011.

Smith, Christian. *Resisting Reagan: The U.S. Central America Peace Movement*. Chicago: University of Chicago Press, 1996.

Smith, Christian, and Amy Adamczyk. *Handing Down the Faith: How Parents Pass Their Religion on to the Next Generation*. New York: Oxford University Press, 2021.

Smith, Christian, and Hilary Davidson. *The Paradox of Generosity: Giving We Receive, Grasping We Lose*. New York: Oxford University Press, 2014.

Smith, Christian, and Michael O. Emerson with Patricia Snell. *Passing the Plate: Why American Christians Don't Give Away More Money*. New York: Oxford University Press, 2008.

Smith, Christian, Kyle Longest, Jonathan Hill, and Kari Christoffersen. *Young Catholic America: Emerging Adults In, Out of, and Gone from the Church*. New York: Oxford University Press, 2014.

Smith, Christian, Bridget Ritz, and Michael Rotolo. *Religious Parenting: Transmitting Faith and Values in Contemporary America*. Princeton, NJ: Princeton University Press, 2020.

Springtide Research Institute. *The State of Religion and Young People: Relational Authority*. Catholic Edition. Winona, MN: Springtide Research Institute, 2020.

Tevington, Patricia. "Americans Feel More Positive Than Negative About Jews, Mainline Protestants, Catholics." Pew Research Center, March 15, 2023. https://www.pewresearch.org/religion/2023/03/15/americans-feel-more-positive-than-negative-about-jews-mainline-protestants-catholics/.

United States Conference of Catholic Bishops. *Ministry to Persons with a Homosexual Inclination*. November 14, 2006. https://www.usccb.org/committees/doctrine/pastoral-care.

U.S. Bishops' Committee on Marriage and Family. *Always Our Children*. A Pastoral Message to Parents of Homosexual Children and Suggestions for Pastoral Ministers. September 10, 1997. https://www.usccb.org/resources/always-our-children.

Vedantam, Shankar. "Where Gratitude Gets You." Interview with David DeSteno. *Hidden Brain*. Podcast audio. No date. https://hiddenbrain.org/podcast/where-gratitude-gets-you.

Wuthnow, Robert. *Sharing the Journey: Support Groups and America's New Quest for Community*. New York: The Free Press, 1996.

Xu, Bin. *The Politics of Compassion: The Sichuan Earthquake and Civic Engagement in China*. Stanford, CA: Stanford University Press, 2017.

Zech, Charles E., Mary L. Gautier, Mark M. Gray, Jonathon L. Wiggins, and Thomas P. Gaunt, SJ, *Catholic Parishes of the 21st Century*. New York: Oxford, 2017.

Index